PRAISE

"A fresh look at the often-mysterious grief dynamics that are universal to the human experience. Drawing from Kubler-Ross's stages of grief (1969), Katie breathes new life and adds depth and modern application including concrete strategies and exercises. Ultimately, we all grieve; here we have illumination for the path. This book offers us hope through normalizing experiences and utilizing them for transformation and growth."

Dr. Johnston Brendel, LPC, LMFT

Counseling Faculty, College of William & Mary

"*The New Face of Grief* arrives at a time when grief is enveloping so many of us in so many different aspects of our lives. This book provides a framework to reflect upon those experiences, create space to process, absorb, feel, pull apart and then put back together the emotions of grief in a growth focused manner—one that breaks down the unhealthy messages many of us have internalized around this universal aspect of life and provides us with healthy and empowering alternatives."

Dr. Carrie Lynn Bailey, LPC, NCC

Clinical Mental Health Counseling Faculty, Walden University

"Katie Rössler has provided us with an expanded model of grief; one which takes into account the major losses in our lives but also, and perhaps most importantly, addresses accumulated losses that can be equally harmful. She raises our awareness of this grief, and by sharing her own journey and the journeys of those she has helped, she provides us with new and effective approach to understand and heal from the grief that has held us back in so many ways. I highly recommend this book to both mental health professionals and those searching for new ways to find greater happiness in their lives."

Rick Gressard, PhD., NCC, LPC

ACA Fellow, William & Mary Chancellor Professor Emeritus

THE NEW FACE OF GRIEF

Transform pain into empowerment

KATIE RÖSSLER, LPC

The New Face of Grief

Print Edition
ISBN: 978-3-9823680-09

Cover design by Jessica Dionne, jessicadionne.com
Images by macrovector
Interior design by Amie McCracken, amiemccracken.com

To my mom: Thank you for the life you lived and for how you raised us.
I miss you beyond words.
To my daughters: May you understand the beauty grief can create in your life.

TABLE OF CONTENTS

PREFACE

The hole. This big open pit inside of us that we try to fill with everything but what it actually needs. The longer it is ignored, the greater impact it has on how we see ourselves, others, and the world around us. A couple years ago, I started noticing the people around me losing faith in themselves. They no longer seemed as strong and able to face whatever life gave them. My counseling clients were talking about life as if they were the victim to it, rather than an active participant. I was hearing things like:

"This woman on the bus made a face at me when I was getting off. I just kept thinking 'Who does she think she is?!? Then on my walk home I realized I left my wallet at the store and had to turn around and catch the next bus. I swear it's like nothing works out for me lately!"

"He doesn't see me anymore! I do everything for him and the kids. I don't even have time to do what I want to or see my friends because everything is about my family. It's like I don't even exist. No thank you. No we appreciate you. Just 'What's for dinner?' or 'Did you wash my shirt I need for tomorrow?'"

We all face different moments in our lives in which life's

challenges compound on top of us and we begin to feel overwhelmed and exhausted. Add the experience of grief to these layers, and we shake our hands at the sky wondering why life is so hard. We stop seeing our role in what is happening in our lives, and we stop listening to our needs. Grief gets amplified as anger, frustration, depression, anxiety, and a sense of emptiness.

When we stop for a moment and reflect on our entire life like a movie, we start to see key pieces of the puzzle that need to be addressed. We remember how frustrations were modeled by others in our lives pointing the finger rather than taking ownership for mistakes. We realize the wounds from a childhood of being treated like we didn't exist by our parents. Once we see all these components in a new way and the grief that we have carried because of them we start to better understand ourselves, our reactions, and where we need to heal.

We start to believe in ourselves again when we notice we have control over how we are impacted by our pasts. In case it hasn't been said to you in a while (or ever): YOU are more than capable of handling anything life brings you, even when you feel like you can't take anymore. The key to knowing this strength inside of you is taking the time to heal from the grief that each death, loss, change, and adaptation created for you.

Most people think of the mud in grief and not the emotions. They think of the darkness, pain, difficulties, and what one might label as suffering. They don't think about the lotus. The growth and beauty that comes only from growing out of dark, murky, and challenging times. We live in a society that runs from these negative, dark emotions and experiences. We want them to be over quickly, with very little effort and only a few side effects. No pressure! Even commercials and billboards want you to believe that buying certain products will relieve these negative emotions quickly. The reality, dear reader, is that the journey of grief cannot be rushed. It does take time and work, but the side effects are pretty amazing when you actually face your grief.

Here we are. The way we are handling grief in our societies, cultures, families, and personal lives is not working for us anymore. To be honest, it hasn't for several generations, which is why we are where we are on this topic. Many of us are suffering and we don't understand it. We are reactive to the ones we love, overwhelmed by life, and feel this fog taking over so much of what used to bring us joy. Grief left alone can cause all of this; however, grief faced can help you enjoy and be present in life in new ways.

You might have already noticed that I am not talking about grief related to death alone. Grief shows up with any major or minor loss or change. This means grief can occur when you move, lose a family member, go to college, get married, change jobs, lose a job, become a parent, experience war...the list could go on. The most widely known example of what can cause grief is the events of 2020 in the world. We all had to change how we went about our day-to-day and how we interacted with each other. It caused and still causes immense grief in so many of us.

Grief is inevitable, so how can we start to experience it differently? What makes some of us go through periods of grief and rise like a phoenix from the ashes while others struggle, diving deep into depression, addiction, or other ways to run from the grief that doesn't go away?

I recently posted in my online community: *True or False: Grief causes suffering.* Most answered true. My heart sank. As I asked for a little more explanation, I started to see why. They labeled the negative emotions and feelings (sadness, anger, hurt, and pain) they experienced for longer periods of time in grief as suffering. I stopped myself from asking them what made these negative emotions last for so long. I believed I already knew the answer after working with clients for twelve years and experiencing my own judgments around grief.

Grief doesn't cause suffering. *We* cause suffering in how we respond to our grief. Grief does cause anger, sadness, anxiety, fear, depression, physical pain, and many other responses linked to these feelings. I will address these throughout this book. The suffering part comes, however, from how we process all these emotions and experiences. It occurs with:

- ✧ How we choose to cope
- ✧ Whether and how we decide to try and run or escape from our emotions
- ✧ Whether or not we can let go of the pain and our expectations of how life should be and find meaning in what has happened

Suffering happens when we struggle to let go of our expectation of how life should look. I don't know about you, but I would rather question my expectations and change them than continue to suffer by staying stuck. Unfortunately, the process isn't as easy.

This book is going to take you on a journey of unlearning false beliefs that impact how you and others experience grief.

It's going to push you to think differently, experience your grief and life in a new way, and help you begin your grief healing journey. Not everything I write will sit well with you, but in those moments, ask yourself: "Is what I am reading uncomfortable because it's striking a chord in me or questioning a belief that I am scared to look at?" I challenge you to take those moments in this book and embrace them. See what you can learn from them. You will come away knowing exactly why you are bothered instead of letting defensiveness win. After all, it's your growth and healing that is the goal.

It's only fair that I share a little about myself now as you will be learning a lot more of my story as you read on. My name is Katie. I am a licensed counselor with over thirteen years' experience working with couples, individuals, and families to help them live healthier and happier lives. Sounds pretty, doesn't it? The reality is that it is not always easy to live a healthier and happier life, especially if it was not modeled for you early on.

These past thirteen years have helped me grow in amazing ways professionally as I worked both with clients in the USA and international clients in Germany where I now live. I have been able to see how much our culture, society, and family impact how we think and react to our life situations. I have also seen how it is quite common in cultures throughout the world to run from grief and find the grief journey uncomfortable.

All therapists know that while life is happening to our clients, life is happening to us as well. The last four years have involved my own grief rollercoaster and have brought me major realizations that have changed how I live life and how I work. In a matter of fourteen months, I lost my mother unexpectedly and had two miscarriages, all while being a wife, mom of two young daughters, adapting to a new country, and running a business. These experiences took me on a road of self-exploration and helped me see that I wasn't new to grief. It had been showing up all throughout my life, but I didn't recognize it because I had the traditional view, as many of us do, that grief was only linked to death.

This book guides you through the journey of learning that there is a new way to look at grief as a tool for growth. Grief shows up more than we realize throughout our lifetime and I hope to help you identify the grief in your own life. Growing up moving every two or three years in a military family, I reflect now and see the grief surrounding each move, each time we had to pull up our roots again and say goodbye to what we knew. My parents' divorce during my teenage years created a grief in me that took years to work through because I didn't understand it. The rite of passage of becoming a mom and a birth experience that almost took my life carried with it grief that I was ashamed to feel but needed to express or it was going to eat me alive. Moving across an ocean, away from everything I knew and understood, to a new country that would become my family's home created a grief of letting go of my vision for life. Not to mention, it kicked up a grief that I didn't expect when I would return home to visit and not feel like I belonged there anymore.

You see, grief shows up throughout our lives because of a variety of situations, not just due to death. It's a normal and natural response to letting go of how we thought life should be and accepting how life is. My hope is that after you read this book you will understand and experience grief in a healthier way that helps you grow. I hope you walk away from this book feeling empowered and capable of facing anything life brings you.

While reading this book, I highly recommend having a pen, pencil, or highlighter nearby, or if the thought of writing in a book makes you anxious (don't worry, you are not alone), grab a journal and take notes. When I read books that hit at key issues I am facing, I find the ability to journal out my thoughts creates even more meaning and greater introspection. This book is going to guide you on your own personal journey, so why not document that as well.

Key Takeaways

- Grief is inevitable.
- Grief can show up in our lives in some big, obvious ways or in some small, undetected, and overlooked ways. However, all grief needs to be faced.
- Grief doesn't need to be scary or avoided.
- There are healthy ways to work through your grief journey instead of running from it.
- The grief healing journey has so many phases and experiences that go along with it. The entire experience leads you to grow into a healthier version of yourself when you allow it to.

It's time to begin your journey by identifying hidden grief in your life and how it is impacting you. These are the first two steps in healing old wounds and discovering how grief can help you grow in beautiful ways.

PART I

GRIEF AS WE KNOW IT

"All the art of living lies in a fine mingling of letting go and holding on."
Havelock Ellis

I have a scientist's brain about the topic of grief. When I see grief in people around me, I pay attention. I study how they talk about what they are experiencing. I notice the symptoms they report having. I recognize the patterns of feeling shame or guilt for what is causing grief in their lives or how they express their grief. It may sound cold, but this is what's going on in the back of my mind. Actively, I listen to their stories and validate their experiences. I explain to them that it's normal to cry in random places, to be triggered by the silliest commercial or song leaving them feeling depressed the rest of the day, or to be super forgetful regularly.

When we grieve, we want to be seen and heard. We don't want to be judged or shamed. We want to feel normal. Sadly, we don't often receive what we want or even need. People don't do this on purpose, at least not usually. It's because of the foundation of beliefs we received about grief from our earliest memories. This forms grief as we know it, and it's important to address the origins of our problems with grief. The following chapters will help you see why we don't always see the grief in our lives, what a new definition of grief can offer us, and how to challenge the old rules of grieving, removing shame and guilt from the process.

CHAPTER 1
THE OCEAN

I feared grief. Mainly because I knew it too well in a very negative light. I knew that in the past, grief led me to break out into hives, have anxiety attacks, and face years of clinical depression and anxiety. I knew that grief could cause people I loved to struggle with addiction, turn towards work to escape, and hurt the people around them because they didn't know how to handle how they felt. It wasn't until the life-changing experience of losing my mom that I learned how to have a different relationship with grief.

I couldn't run away from grief this time. Losing a mom unexpectedly while being a mom to two young girls wasn't going to let me ignore or avoid my feelings any longer. I felt grief daily as I mothered my daughters. I was faced with it directly when my daughters had questions about their grandmother or I wanted to call her for advice. If I didn't learn to see grief in a new way, it would have a lasting impact on how my kids responded to grief in the future too. I was determined and completely uncertain how to navigate the waters of my own personal grief. So my journey began.

MY STORY

Grief became familiar to me as a kid. We moved every two or three years because my dad was in the military. Sometimes we would find out only months before the move where we were going. As a kid, I hated it so much. Now I look back and see how it helped me grow into the counselor and woman I am today. Here were my stages of grief with each move:

Denial: There's no way I am moving again!

Bargaining: If I am really good, can we stay here, pretty please?

Anger: I hate you all! This is unfair!

Sadness: All the tears, all the time.

Acceptance: Ok fine! I will go make new friends and try to like this place. Give me the biggest bedroom in our new house, and I'll get adjusted even faster!

Then there was my parents' separation and divorce. That occurred over the ages of thirteen to fifteen years old. Talk about a fun time. We'll leave it at that...but again grief, a grief that lasted for years and still at times impacts my marriage now. Next was going to college. Say what you want, but I think most people go through a period of grief starting in a new place. Even an exciting rite of passage like going to college can come with grief as you get adjusted to being more independent. Throughout those college years, I had relationships and break-ups of my own. Grief again. Hurricane Katrina changed the landscape of my extended family's home where I spent my summers. The impact of the places you loved in your childhood no longer existing is a huge shock to the system and can create its own grief.

I went off to get my masters and during that time ended a long-term relationship and almost lost my father due to a complication in surgery. All of that was within two months of each other. Talk about an existential crisis of what is up and what is down and "oh wait, the people I love won't live forever?" This was the point in my life where I really didn't deal with grief well. I tried to avoid the waves of grief but ended up spiraling down a hole that I created, all the while thinking I was escaping it. Drinking, an unhealthy relationship, and avoiding my real responsibilities became my distracters but actually were making things worse for me.

I grew up a lot after that, working my first two jobs, living on my own, and meeting my husband. When you partner with someone and decide to spend the rest of your lives together, *all* your baggage shows up. Anything unresolved gets a huge magnifying glass focused on it, and you realize that you both have a lot of healing and learning to do. A year after being married, I became a mom, and yep, grief showed up there too. Because of a traumatic, near-death experience giving birth, I grieved for over a year. I went into my pregnancy with the "of course everything will be fine" mentality, and it stayed that way until a few days before my daughter's due date. HELLP syndrome hit my body hard and fast without warning. I had skipped the chapters and online articles about C-sections because I didn't plan for that to be my story. There was no other option once I was in the hospital, and I was left feeling like I hadn't really given birth because I didn't get to choose the method of delivery.

Then there was moving to a new country—my husband's home country—and having our second child there only a few months after we arrived. All this while trying to set up a new home, help a toddler adjust to learning a new language, and figuring out a new culture. Easy, right? There it was again: grief, grief, grief. My grandfather died a couple days after my second daughter was born without getting to meet her virtually. I still feel the frustration and guilt with myself for not trying harder to connect, but we didn't know we were going to lose him. This guilt that comes up I realize I am conditioned to feel as a woman. I "should" have thought of it all even though I was newly out of the hospital and recovering from birth. I see the silliness in this expectation, and yet the guilt is still there. A year later, I experienced grief related to reverse culture shock when I visited home. My own culture no longer felt like home. I felt like I didn't make sense in my culture anymore. Where was my home now?

All this grief was starting to stack up like pancakes! Little did I know that it was about to be compounded by a boulder of loss that I could never have imagined.

In 2018 came the biggest impact on my life. I lost my mom. It's funny how I wrote that. I "lost" my mom, like she could be found again. For my own grief process, I will rewrite that now: my mom died in 2018 unexpectedly.

I was a mom without a mom.

No longer could I call her to ask, "Was I like this as a kid?" or get advice about parenting and tools for my own sanity. She was gone, and it shocked my system like jumping into a freezing cold mountain lake.

Nine months later, I experienced my first miscarriage when I was eight weeks along and then six months later another miscarriage. I started 2020 with a goal for myself (as if I could control this): "I will not be told 'I am so sorry' at all this year." Well 2020 came, and I think the whole world was saying "I am so sorry" to each other. So much for my goal! Don't worry, I say that with laughter now.

I don't write all this to impress you or overwhelm you. I write all this to say it wasn't until this last year that it all clicked about what grief really is. I realized that I and most of the world had been grieving in a really unhealthy way for a long time. When I would grieve in the past, I would spend money I didn't really have, avoid difficult conversations with people that needed to happen for me to move on, and party with friends acting like everything was ok. I didn't know how to grieve in healthy ways or even how to begin the healing process. If you look back, you will see I have a lifetime of experiences where grief showed up, and I didn't have a clue how to handle it until now. So, if you are looking at your life and judging yourself for not seeing your grief more clearly, there is absolutely no reason to. Sometimes it doesn't click until all of a sudden you wake up and you see your experience through a new lens. What's important is that you start the journey of looking at grief differently.

After my mom died, I began to see grief as this deep, dark ocean. Water has always been soothing to me, but this body of water created fear in me of being overtaken. I was determined, though, that I would not allow it to drown me like it had in the past. This time I would allow grief to swallow me up and see what happened without panicking or running. What I learned was that grief doesn't swallow you up at all. It may feel like that initially, but that's just the fear talking. Grief holds you, rocks you, and helps you grow in incredible ways when you finally dive in.

So, that's what I did. I jumped into this deep, dark ocean of emotions. I visualized myself sinking into it, deeper and deeper until I just seemed to float in the middle of it. I wasn't drowning at all. I could feel myself safely cocooned deep in grief. I could breathe and feel safe. This began my new relationship with a process I used to run away from. Grief became a tool to help me grow and a beautiful experience that continues to shape me. I am regularly being soothed and smoothed out like a rock in water. It doesn't always feel good, but I learned to fight it a lot less so that I don't suffer because of my own stubbornness or desire to avoid negative emotions.

WE ALL GET STUCK

Let me make it clear that we all get stuck in grief at some point. It wasn't until early 2020 that I realized a part of me was still stuck in the emergency room right after I found out my first daughter needed to come out via an emergency C-section or I would not survive. Almost five years later, that grief reawakened during my first miscarriage in 2019 when I was lying on a bed in an operating room again. It hit me like a ton of bricks because I had not worked through the grief of my first birth experience. My body and mind were still stuck in that initial trauma.

For over five years, I thought my impatience and quickness to get stressed out were just a "normal" part of being a mom. Well, yes and no. Largely, however, a part of me still held on to that traumatic moment and never actually grieved or healed.

Never finding the bigger meaning or purpose in that event was holding me back. I didn't allow myself to feel all the emotions because now I was a mom. But wasn't that what I had always wanted? This false belief system that "I got what I wanted, so why was I so upset?" kept me stuck. You will learn later on in the book about how to knock down the old ways of thinking about grief, but I encourage you to reflect now on what experiences and situations you have had where you may still be stuck.

It may have to hit you like a ton of bricks to realize what it is, like it did me, or it may take some time to reflect over a few days to get some clarity. Hopefully, all it takes is reflecting on this question and allowing your body, mind, and emotions to speak up. Our bodies store our stories. By taking time to tune in to what stories need some tending and resolution, we can see the grief work that still needs to be done. Sometimes this means an afternoon of crying and other times it means weeks or months of focused work to finally release areas that have been stuck for years.

I will tell you this: I have yet to meet someone in my personal and professional life who actively worked on their grief and regretted it. No one has ever said to me, "I suffer because I did grief work." I hear the opposite: "I never faced my grief, and I have been suffering because of it. Now I feel like a weight has lifted off of me." Grief's bad reputation leaves people with years of running away from thoughts and feelings that tend to be misunderstood. I believe once you integrate your grief into who you are, it is as simple and as powerful as breathing.

Key Takeaways

- ✧ Grief adds up over time without us even realizing it. Taking time to reflect on your life story and how grief has impacted it can help you to see what still needs to be healed.
- ✧ Having an analogy for your grief, like a deep, dark ocean, can help you better visualize your experience and even shift your view of it, giving you more control.
- ✧ It is normal to experience being stuck in grief, as most of us were not shown how to handle grief in healthy ways. Recognize that normal "stressed out" responses can be related to grief.

CHAPTER 2

HIDDEN GRIEF

Why a new face of grief? Because how we live our lives, avoiding grief and sometimes not even recognizing it, isn't working for us anymore. I watch people daily both in person and online struggling because they haven't faced old grief from life challenges and losses. They fill their schedules full, stay in a place of urgency in their lives, and find coping skills that weigh them down instead of actually relieving them. Have you noticed how being busy is sometimes seen as having it all together? It's definitely not the case when we are running from grief, but others don't get to see that. We are rewarded for our avoiding with compliments of how much we are doing and how well we seem to be.

It's time we start to wake up to the unresolved grief that is in our lives so we can take action to heal it. I have been gathering stories from people who have faced grief in their lives and found meaning (you'll see them sprinkled throughout this book) and even just sharing about gathering these stories has opened people's eyes to how many life events can and have brought about grief. Grief tends to be an experience linked with physical loss and death. This is where we get it wrong. Grief shows up often in our lives and is a completely normal response. It can be small and last for a week or so, or it can take time to unravel and process.

You probably know grief really well, but you may not have realized that's what it was if you have:

- lost a job or a home.
- experienced war in any form.
- had a loss of someone you love.
- had a miscarriage or lost a baby.
- gone through a natural disaster.
- had a dream that was not fulfilled for your child or for yourself.
- gone through a separation or divorce.
- moved to a new country or gone through reverse culture shock.
- experienced a major move, change, or a rite of passage that created a significant change in your life.
- changed something in your identity...even if it was a "good" thing like getting married or becoming a parent.
- experienced a change in health status or chronic illness.
- had someone you love disclose a new identity from how you knew them.
- disclosed aspects of your identity to others after a long time living as they thought you should.
- ended a significant relationship or relationships to form healthier boundaries for yourself.

I bet you could add to this list with some of your own experiences too.

Dr. Kenneth Doka, a professor and grief specialist, calls grief that isn't typically acknowledged by our society as disenfranchised grief. Because society won't acknowledge your grief, it doesn't give *you* space to acknowledge and process it. This leads to you not acknowledging that what you are experiencing is, in fact, grief. Instead, you experience tension in your body, headaches and migraines, digestion issues, sleep issues, addiction, emotional outbursts, and mental health issues. This grief, that I like to call hidden grief, goes untreated and leads to us feeling overwhelmed and unhappy in life.

All of the above examples involve expectations that life will go one way but then there is a shift. A complete 180 at times. Something doesn't go as planned, or as we thought it should. When I became a mother, I didn't realize how much I would grieve my old life. Even now with three kids, I miss those days of freedom and flexibility. I grieve the loss of my old identity. It doesn't mean I am not grateful for my kids or the life I live. You can be grateful *and* grieve. I'll share more on that later in the book.

> Often guilt keeps us from giving ourselves permission to grieve.

We can often trace back to our childhoods to see how we were taught to handle grief. Whether we follow in our family members' footsteps or go the complete opposite way, it's not often we can separate ourselves from what was modeled for us growing up. That includes how each phase of grief was handled. I grew up in a family where appearances mattered for a variety of reasons. When grief showed up, there were as a woman really only two acceptable phases beyond acceptance—bargaining and depression—and they were not allowed to last very long. You may have grown up with anger being normal as well, but in my family, we tended to suffer in silence.

I have learned now that it's a generational problem when we struggle to express grief in healthy ways. Generations before us have been uncertain how to let their emotions out in the context of their culture, family, and society. They themselves were forced into the box of how people did things and many of them passed that along to their kids whether they meant to or not. So here we are, generations later, all acting like we are just fine, or struggling to get out of bed and function, or standing face to face with addiction. The reality is we are not ok, and it's time to face what's going on.

SO, WHY A NEW FACE OF GRIEF?

Because we deserve to be complex, beautiful human beings who can handle a variety of thoughts and emotions. We deserve to know how strong we actually are and to believe in our ability to overcome the natural struggles of life. We deserve to be able to grieve, no matter what the situation, without judgment or rules. We deserve to know how going through grief in healthy ways can help us grow so that we can stop running from grief.

We also need to change the definition of grief so that we

don't assume it only relates to death or physical loss. By keeping the old definition, we walk around experiencing something and not knowing what to call it. Have you ever watched a young child figure out the word for something they are feeling? Their eyes get really big and they feel validated. "You are really *angry* that John took your toy." "Yes! I am angry!" We need that big-eyed validation that what we are feeling has a definition and is something that we can work on.

A friend called me after I shared that I was collecting stories of meaning from people's experiences with grief. She seemed to be in a state of shock mixed with excitement. "Katie, I read the list of life experiences where grief can show up, and it hit me: I have needed to grieve our move and to let go of how I thought life would look for years now but was afraid to because I didn't understand what it was about. I just need to grieve! Thank you!" She wasn't the first to share a similar realization after I started sharing about the project. We all need validation for these unknown, ambiguous feelings that we have. The reality is they feel unknown and ambiguous because the current definition of grief stops us from fully seeing it. It's time to change this.

Key Takeaways

- ✧ Grief shows up for us through positive and negative experiences throughout our lives, not just death.
- ✧ We can be grateful and grieve. We can be grateful for what we have and grieve what we

don't have or what has changed.

- The current definition of grief and what society has taught us about grief has stopped many of us from realizing when grief is showing up in our lives.

CHAPTER 3

THE RULES OF GRIEF

Have you ever sat and thought about how many rules are connected to grief? Often, we become impatient with grief and ourselves because we have the shoulds of grief stuck in our minds:

This shouldn't take so long.

This shouldn't look this way.

Grief should last no more than a year.

You should be over it by now.

You should cry a lot when grieving.

You aren't crying enough.

You shouldn't cry too much.

You should stay busy when grieving.

You shouldn't be too busy.

You should take time off.

You should move on.

You shouldn't move on—it's too soon.

We have created a box for how grief should look and how we are allowed to respond. Funnily enough, we tend to contradict ourselves with our rules. Cry but don't cry too much. Stay busy but also take time to grieve. Move on but not too soon. We are excellent at being hypocritical with grief as well. Our rules don't necessarily apply to others and vice versa. I may tell a friend "take all the time you need to grieve" but then get annoyed at myself for still grieving. Someone might tell you it's time to move on but get angry when someone gives them the same "advice" during their process.

When we go through something that means grief will be knocking at our door, we want to turn and run away. It's no wonder. There are too many rules for a concept that is so subjective! It's time to put an end to the rules of grief.

When we stop telling ourselves the way to grieve and how long it should take, we free ourselves from expectations that tend to be false and keep us stuck. I remember being told, "The first year of grieving a death is the hardest." A whole year! It was like having a death sentence of my own. Yes, the first year was tough, but the second year was too. I went into the first year with horrible expectations based on what I was told and wasn't prepared for the way grief actually showed up in my life. Christmas came, and I held my breath the whole day. What I found was the day itself was not so bad. My family and I stayed busy with events all day, and my kids kept me laughing and playing. It was the days following that which were less eventful that were the toughest. I expected the anniversary of my mom's death to be a horrible day in bed. I felt such peace that day. However, it was the week before that was the hardest as I anticipated what that day would be like. The anxiety of how it would feel was often worse than what I actually felt on an anniversary or holiday.

What changed after the first year of my mother's death was that I went into it with way more empowerment because I understood grief differently. I understood what made me sad or angry in the process, and I wasn't afraid of grief anymore. I understood what still caused my heart to stop and panic to set in, and I knew ways to help calm myself down. I didn't need to go through the first year of grief to learn healthy ways to grieve. Had I already known healthier ways to grieve, the first year would have come with just as much beauty as pain. I wouldn't have held my breath so much but would have trusted myself and my ability to experience (notice I didn't say handle) what was to come.

The rules of grief don't work for me anymore, and I hope they won't work for you anymore either. What if we wrote new rules for grief that gave us the freedom to experience it in our own way:

You are allowed to grieve in any way you want that is safe.

You are allowed to take time off or keep working...and that decision can change day to day.

You are allowed to wear all black or the brightest colors in your wardrobe to express how you feel.

You are allowed to cry every day, scream in anger, want to break something, want to run, want to escape, want to stay in bed for weeks, or say no to every invitation to be social.

On the flip side, here would be my rules for what *not to do* when grieving:

YOU ARE NOT ALLOWED TO ACTIVELY HURT YOURSELF OR OTHERS.

This may still happen from time to time, but it means not actively causing physical and emotional harm to others or yourself. For some, the pain of grief is so great at times that we can become aggressive: hitting walls or ourselves, cutting ourselves, or attacking others. We can cause physical pain by starving ourselves or overeating to the point of sickness. Even drinking or overmedicating can cause harm to yourself and others. We can lash out at others, either with physical violence or emotional violence by mocking the care offered to us or withholding love from our loved ones.

We can become so upset, leading us to do things to ourselves or others that we wouldn't normally do. Calling people names, being vindictive, and saying things to hurt others so they feel some bit of what we feel are other ways we can cause emotional pain in others. Now, these are extreme cases, but it's best we don't just focus on the lighter emotions of grief. We need to address the fact that we weren't always taught healthy ways to grieve, so we may not always act in the healthiest (or smartest) ways either.

YOU ARE NOT ALLOWED TO LEAVE YOUR LIFE AND LOVED ONES BEHIND.

This hits on two things: suicide and escape. Thoughts of suicide can be high during times of grief when we feel hopeless and helpless. The issue is how far down the rabbit hole we allow our thoughts to go. When this has happened to me in the past, I have responded by reaching out to a support person or group to keep me above water. You can find a therapist, coach, doctor, friend, or family member to be your point of contact that you check-in with regularly. The key is when your thoughts head in the direction of ending your life, *reach out for help*.

The other area this hits on is escaping. This always makes me think of the stereotypical midlife crisis (which, by the way, involves grieving too!): buying a new, expensive car; changing your wardrobe; or leaving your family behind. It's hard for the person to accept life as it is, and they want to revisit the good ole days of their younger years or how life would be without responsibilities. They run away from what's right in front of them (usually a family or career) because they struggle to grieve the fact that life has changed and may not be exactly what they wanted it to be.

Don't run away from what's in your life. You can see that changes need to be made, but a hasty cut off from life as you know it isn't typically a healthy way to respond in grief. It impacts you and those around you in huge ways.

YOU ARE NOT ALLOWED TO IGNORE YOUR OWN NEEDS WHILE YOU ARE GRIEVING.

Each grief experience is unique. Everyone grieves differently and even the same person will have a different way of grieving different kinds of loss. The next step would be addressing what *you* need while grieving. Here are some needs that I see being particularly important:

You need to make time weekly if not daily to grieve in a way that helps you.

You need to have one or two people to talk to about your grief who know how to be there for you.

You need to find coping skills that are not food, alcohol, drugs, shopping, etc. to work through the emotions grief creates for you.

You need to make space for anniversaries to allow grief to happen...even ten years later.

You need to give yourself grace and step outside of the rule box society wants to put you in...even if that means confronting family, friends, coworkers, your boss, or looking in the mirror and addressing yourself. You are your own advocate as you go through your grieving process.

I am basically asking you to rewrite how you were explicitly and implicitly taught about grief throughout your life. I realize that's a tall order. It doesn't change in a day but shifts gradually as you notice more and more how you want to see and experience grief in your life. Be gentle with yourself. When I work with clients to decondition false beliefs around grief it usually involves facing childhood messages that lead to a lot of emotions. You don't have to go on this part of the journey alone, but it is a crucial first building block that must occur.

Address the old rules, create your new rules, set boundaries on what you don't want to do and then list your needs in grief. These tasks help you get a better picture and plan for your grief as you embark on your healing journey.

Key Takeaways

- ✧ Our culture, society, and even family create rules we accept to be true about grief, which can impact our ability to grieve in healthy ways.
- ✧ It is important that we define our own rules for grieving, as well as what we need during our grief process.
- ✧ Remember you are your greatest advocate. Speak up when you feel like you are being boxed in by someone else's rules.
- ✧ Create your picture of grief with a healthier plan by confronting the old rules, writing new rules, knowing your boundaries, and making your needs clear.

PART 2
THE PHASES OF GRIEF

"In Louisiana, one of the first stages of grief is eating your weight in Popeyes fried chicken. The second stage is doing the same with boudin. People have been known to swap the order. Or to do both at the same time."
Ken Wheaton, Sweet as Cane, Salty as Tears

The phases, or stages, of grief create mixed feelings in people. Some love them as a guide for what they are going through. Others believe they lack a lot of the complexities of what we experience. I am in the middle. I believe they give us an interesting framework, and they help us begin to normalize and connect.

You'll find later in the book I talk about the other experiences of grief, but for now, looking at these phases and better understanding what is going on in each is helpful. I challenge you to look at each phase with the intention of better understanding the human experience of grief. Why do we go through the emotions we do? What causes us to act or react when triggered? How does our brain believe it is protecting us during the grief process?

When we come to the table as a student of grief, we learn so much more, than if we come ready to debate what is right or wrong. I choose to see the phases as the potential floorplan of grief in which the actual building may look somewhat different once completed. The following chapters are written with this mindset, and I share my own experiences as well as past clients' (with permission to share of course). These phases are not a rule of how grief will look or even what order they will occur. The order I chose to teach about each is based on how you typically learn about the stages of grief.

While reading each, reflect on your past related to grief and how you may have journeyed through some or all of these phases.

CHAPTER 4

DENIAL: A CHILD'S GAME

Hey Katie's brain,

I know what you're doing. We can play pretend for as long as you want, but we both know the truth. You're hiding from the feelings you don't want to address. You keep filling your schedule, saying "no" to you while saying "yes" to everyone else. But the longer you run, the bigger the emotions you're trying to avoid will feel. When you're ready, I promise you can handle what will come. I'll just stand by till you empty your schedule for...you.

Love,

Your Inner Voice

Have you ever seen a toddler cover their face and say "You can't see me" and really believe it only because they can't see you? I laugh at this analogy because it's exactly what we do when facing grief. "If I cover my eyes then I can't see you, so you can't see me, Grief." If I don't acknowledge the loss or life challenge, then it never really happened...right? Well, we all know the answer to this, but yet we still cover our eyes and play the game.

Denial is powerful and makes us feel like we have control. The night before the anniversary of my mom's death, I cover my eyes. I refuse to go to sleep. It happens every year. This little voice starts saying to me: "If you don't go to sleep then the anniversary won't happen and it won't be real." I fall for it every time and find myself staying up till 11:58 p.m. I cry each year because I know even if I don't go to sleep, 12:01 a.m. will still happen, and another year will have passed without her on this earth. There is no way to stop time, and honestly, there is no point. Denial is powerful, and that little kid in us covers our eyes to play the game so that we don't have to face the painful reality.

During the first year anniversary after playing the game with my grief, I eventually went to sleep with a puffy face and runny nose. The next day I woke up early with my daughters and played a slideshow of my mom's life from her funeral that the girls had never seen. Pictures from her childhood doing activities that my girls love to do now made them smile and giggle. My heart was so full of joy bringing them this confirmation that they were like their grandmother. I also experienced sadness that she wasn't there to tell them the stories from these pictures that I would never know the details to tell. I felt a sense of calm with both emotions and wondered why on earth I had let denial back into my mind.

The next year, I felt the build up, and there was the denial again. I stayed up, cried a ton, and then woke up feeling a huge weight lifted off my shoulders. I realized that it was part of my healing journey to remember that it is ok that mom is no longer here and that as hard as the reality is, life goes on in beautiful ways when I stop fighting it. Maybe next year I'll go to sleep on time, or maybe not, but now I know the anniversary day isn't the hardest for me, it's the day before that is. The day denial rears its ugly head and tries to take control.

THE TWO DS: DODGEBALL AND DENIAL

I was talking to a friend recently about the phase of denial in grief and how funny it can be when we look at it objectively. She shared about her four-year-old son who likes to play a lot. When he knows he is doing something wrong and sees you about to respond, he gets in a position like playing dodgeball, ready to deflect anything you are going to say or do. His mom shared it's hard not to laugh at it when he starts to physically dodge back and forth when she says things like "please clean up the mess you left on the floor." She started laughing as she shared the story and showed me his "moves," and I realized how much denial is exactly like playing a game of dodgeball with reality. "You can't get me!" "You missed again Grief, haha!" "I'm too fast for you!" Eventually, we get hit by the ball and most of the time it doesn't feel that good.

> Denial is a child's game. Acceptance is showing we are ready to grow up and face reality.

It's easy to write a sentence like this, but let's talk about why our brain goes into dodgeball mode after finding out something has changed in our lives. Our brain's desire is to keep things simple and status quo, even if it isn't the best for us. It goes into self-protection mode thinking it is helping us. We don't want our view of the world to change, so our brain denies its reality. In this case then, denial is normal and part of the progression toward acceptance. However, when we stay stuck in the dodgeball game, we give this phase of grief more power than it needs to have.

Someone asked me the other day, "How can we really know if we are in denial so we can get ourselves out of it?" Great question! I wish I had a one-size-fits-all answer. However, it's subjective because everyone experiences the phase of denial in a different way. Some of us have a self-awareness that helps us recognize denial a bit faster than others so we can start to talk ourselves back into reality. Others of us will have friends or family point things out to us, and if we find we are reacting emotionally, like getting defensive or offended, it gives us a warning sign that we probably are in denial. Then there is the group of deniers who stay stuck in their denial, which blocks them from confronting the truth of their situation and moving toward healing, and this can be tough, as an onlooker, to watch.

Depending on the situation, we can all fall into any of these groups—sometimes you may be self-aware, sometimes you'll be able to react to and handle the truth from a loved one, and sometimes you may get stuck in denial, which can have a serious impact on those who care about you. I have worked with several couples who went through the experience of one of them being in complete denial and not ready to face reality. I ended up working with the other partner on how to be patient and prepared for when their partner did eventually face the truth. It can be hard on both partners in a relationship when one is stuck in denial, but one cannot push or nag their partner out of denial.

THE MIND-BODY CONNECTION

Let's talk about how denial can impact our bodies. Have you ever held in a negative emotion, like frustration, so others could not see it? It almost builds and builds till it finds a way out. This can be in an emotional outburst or in physical symptoms. We have learned the negative impacts of stress on our bodies over the past few years as more and more people are facing burnout. Indeed found that burnout rates have increased almost nine percent since before 2020 to 2021. Staying in denial can create some similar symptoms. It is like placing emotional stress on your mind and body, but the state of denial keeps us from fully realizing that we, ourselves, are causing these problems.

I remember the first time I broke out into hives. It was the first Christmas after my parents separated and my dad, brother, and I were spending a few days with his side of the family. I felt the tension around me as a young teenager, but everyone was acting like everything was ok. After a day or two, the itchiness began. It showed up at its worst at night when I finally had time to stop acting like I was ok. Lying there, miserable, it was like all of my emotions were coming to the surface. An anger, a fire, inside of me that wanted to come out to say this was not fair, not right, and no one should be acting like things were normal. Things were not normal!

We went to a doctor because the hives got so bad, but no one addressed the elephant in the room. No one asked me if I was ok or what might be causing it. I was given some cream, directions for when to apply it, and was sent back home. Looking back, I realize my family was doing the best they could in an awkward and uncomfortable situation. They wanted my brother and me to feel normal, to feel loved, but ignoring what was changing in our world made me feel more isolated. I was too young to understand fully what was happening to me, but now I look back and see how denial, even the denial of others around me, was impacting me physically in a really uncomfortable way.

It's undeniable that our minds and bodies are connected. Research shows this time and time again. Our thoughts affect our posture. Our beliefs impact our body's ability to fight off sicknesses. Denial creates a container in our minds that leads our bodies to respond "Help me!" It's up to us to listen.

IT'S A FAMILY THING

Unfortunately, it was modeled for me early on in my family to act like everything was okay, even if inside of me I was screaming out for help. Slap on top of that being the first-born who was the classic hero-child (most of the time), and the pressure to always be happy was stronger than ever. My focus was on making sure I didn't do anything wrong, no matter what was going on around me. As I got older, that turned into escaping and denying the real impact events had on me. Even when people finally acknowledged something must have been difficult for me, I would downplay or deflect by saying things were harder for someone else. Denial is a powerful tool. Our brains can convince us so easily that we are not affected at all by our world tumbling down around us.

Growing up in a family of people who emotionally struggle with boundaries can lead a child to hold in their own issues. A dad who reacts in anger at anything that doesn't go his way. A mom who could have her own soap opera based on her reactions to anyone who doesn't receive her with positivity and open arms. These reactive parents make it unsafe for a kid to express themselves, and so they don't. The parents take up all the emotional space. The children grow up learning to deny their feelings, to the point of convincing themselves.

Or you could have grown up with emotionally healthy parents who communicated what was going on and talked about challenges as a family, but due to your personality type you may not have been as comfortable with this. It was easier to deny that you had an issue than have to talk it to pieces in the next family meeting. This makes total sense, especially in the teenage years, but over time, it also teaches you that denial is an acceptable form of coping so you don't have to talk about what's really going on.

These are all potential scenarios for how easy it is to learn denial as a part of a coping mechanism. If you read these and say "yep, that's me" or it makes you think of your own family situation that made denial easy to use, do not worry. This habit can be unlearned or as we like to say now adays "deconditioned." It takes a higher level of awareness, obviously, but this can also happen. The key is wanting to change it, recognizing your cycle of response that ends in denial, and seeing where in the cycle you can start making changes.

DO WE REALLY NEED TO RUN?

The outcomes of denial are endless and typically lead to health issues, both mental and physical. People are experiencing migraines, ulcers, insomnia, depression, anxiety, panic attacks, hives, eating problems, addictions, and emotional outbursts with little to no clue that grief is causing it. Our healthcare and prescription medicine bills rack up, and we are left not knowing exactly what the problem is because we are in denial of the impact of grief in our lives.

When we seek to escape the loss, adjustment, and changes we are facing, we do a lot of damage to ourselves. Addictions get fed (abusing alcohol or drugs or excessive working, exercising, food, shopping, etc.), our bodies cry out with health conditions, and we slowly create more issues and challenges for ourselves than if we would just face the monster under our bed. The grief isn't doing this. We are doing this to ourselves. We believe that by escaping and denying it, it won't be real. We won't have to feel the sadness, fear, anger, or disappointment—or acceptance. And by thinking we are escaping, we pile on even more negativity into our lives.

The real question is, when did we stop believing in our ability to handle the normal parts of life? When did so many cultures around the world start to shift from reality to the fake Hollywood facade of life? We went from: we will experience loss in our lives in some form or fashion, we will all die, pain is normal and can be relieved in healthy ways. To: avoid grief, loss, and pain at all costs; don't talk about it; sink further into addiction; distract; and run. How did this happen? I could blame marketing and movies, but the reality is, our own fears about the unknown took over. We are talking about generations upon generations who struggled to understand grief as a normal and natural part of life. It leads one to wonder when did this shift begin?

The Mexican holiday Day of the Dead honors those who have died and normalizes death as a part of life. Native Americans have long understood loss, change, and death as a normal part of life and have rituals to honor each. Many cultures have celebrations and ceremonies for rites of passage to shed light on the fact that these changes can be impactful and can cause growth and adjustment. Though traditions are there for some, most of us still feel stuck in how to handle grief, which leads us down the path that seems the easiest: denial.

A person loses a job and feels shame, causing them to avoid the feelings about losing stability in their lives. They turn to drinking, spending money that they need to be saving, or struggling to get out of bed each day. Facing their grief seems unbearable and running away from it the only option. We escape because we believe on a primal level that facing reality—facing the pain—will kill us, and we want to avoid death. Pain, both physical and emotional, creates fear in us, which kicks up our caveman brain that says, "Stay alive at all costs! Run, fight, avoid!"

Denial originally started out as a way to help us cope with the reality of our mortality, but now it has been twisted to cope with anything we are not happy with in our lives: a death, a loss, a change, an inability to go back to how it was. If we don't want to feel it or think about it, our brains know what to do. Here's the thing: I believe there is a point where either we look in the mirror and say "No more running" or our loved ones intervene, and we finally listen. Denial won't last forever, and if you are actively aware that you want to work on your grief, it's less likely to be a stage you journey through very intensely.

Key Takeaways

- ✧ Denial is our brain's way of protecting us from the pain of things changing.
- ✧ Denying our grief can cause physical and mental health problems if we stay in this phase too long.
- ✧ Denial can be learned from our families as the way to deal with grief.
- ✧ Our brains have long been conditioned for denial when it comes to the reality of our mortality. Over time we have twisted denial into a negative coping mechanism for any change we don't want to experience.

CHAPTER 4.5
OUR ADDICTION TO ESCAPING

Before we move to another phase of grief, I want to address the unspoken truth about when we try to escape grief, whether it be because of denial or because we are fully aware that we don't want to feel the emotions that come with grief. We can easily fall into something I like to call escape addiction. Like any other addiction, it's seductive and can swallow you up before you realize it. Shauna Niequist explained this in her book *Present Over Perfect*. She shares that a drug can be created out of anything you want. It's how you use it. Think of it as whatever you do to numb out or disconnect from your reality. I reflected on my own use of my phone, working extra hours, and volunteering for too many things! Shauna warns that the more that we use our "drug of choice" the easier it is to separate ourselves from the things that hold value to us. This includes the people we love and taking care of ourselves.

Escape addiction is when we pursue activities that are ultimately unhealthy, though they may seem healthy at first, to avoid facing our grief. The act of escape is what is addicting.

Mine in the last year has been binge watching different shows. I told myself it was me making time for myself. I was allowing myself to unwind and relax. It got to the point that one, rare kid-free weekend, I went into total binge mode and thought to myself "What are you doing? You could actually be taking care of yourself right now, but instead you are watching a ton of TV." You might be thinking, "But what's wrong with that?" Nothing, unless it's an escape addiction, like it turned into for me because it's not normal for me to watch so much TV. I was definitely avoiding healthier ways of taking care of myself and the feelings that come with acknowledging my grief.

I called up a friend and told her what was going on. I let it out: "I feel stuck in my grief." There it was, the elephant in the room, and I was the only one sitting next to it. I was trying to escape the thing that I talk to so many about not escaping. The next morning, I took a walk by myself along a nearby river. I didn't really want to go for that walk. There was a voice in me that said, "No, stay! Watch the next episode and find out what happens to so-and-so and the new drama that's about to come." It felt like ropes had been tied around me to keep me on the couch, but my brain and my heart realized I had to break free of them.

On my walk, I stopped and sat on a bench. The sky was full of beautiful white clouds, and as I stared at them, I got a clear message of what was really going on. "Katie, you are escaping and it's become addictive." When reality hits us, sometimes it's inspirational and sometimes it's humbling. This was one of the latter times. It was humbling to realize that I was falling into what so many do as well: escape addiction.

It was so easy to disguise it as self-care, "me" time, doing something I wanted to do in all the hustle and bustle of family life, but what was really happening was that I wanted to escape. Screen time (TV, cell phones, computers, tablets) is addictive. The research is clear about this. It hits the pleasure center of the brain, just like gambling, sex, or drugs. So, I was falling into an addiction with screens that I was justifying to myself in order to escape what I was really feeling.

Brene Brown wrote in her book *Daring Greatly* about three types of escape mechanisms we use. The first type is the behaviors that lead to addiction I mentioned in the previous chapter: drugs, alcohol, shopping, eating, etc. The second is perfectionism which keeps us from facing reality by attempting to control as much as possible to a fault. The last escape mechanism is one I am very familiar with. It's the inability to enjoy the moment in front of us because we believe something bad will happen to us. I have long said to my husband that when things are going well I always expect something bad to happen. I actually can start to get uncomfortable when everything is going well. This leads me to not be able to enjoy the present as much and escape the reality that the other shoe isn't dropping right now...and that's ok! By escaping the enjoyment of the moment, I am preparing myself for the bad that is destined to come so that it doesn't hurt me as much. Anyone else see how messed up this thinking is?

Escape addiction hurts us just like any other addiction because it makes us believe what we are doing is better than what we need to face. It secretly whispers in our ears that we can't handle the negative emotions that need to be felt. It makes us think less of ourselves and our capabilities. It's a seduction that says, "You don't really want to feel all those horrible emotions. Come do this instead. You'll feel so much better..." I am here to tell you that this is not true. Short-term gratification on a regular basis kicks at our ability to endure challenging situations. You were made to be able to handle anything that comes your way, but you have been conditioned to believe otherwise.

PROCRASTINATION AT ITS FINEST

The reality is that escaping is a form of procrastination. When we procrastinate, we believe we are protecting ourselves from something super unpleasant that we need to do. What we are actually doing is making things worse by not completing the task as soon as possible. We cause our suffering by pushing off the task, but we convince ourselves that we are helping by prolonging the inevitable of what needs to be done. We suffer with the dread of an unpleasant task for much longer than it would take to actually complete the task itself.

Escape addiction is when that procrastination, that enjoyment of escaping, becomes mixed with an addictive behavior that is hard to break. Like I shared before, mine is screen time: on my phone, computer, or television. It sucks me in, and I believe I am doing something good for myself, when in reality increased screen time leads to depression, anxiety, insomnia, and a variety of other mental and physical health issues. The longer and more regularly you use your "drug of choice" to escape, the more uncomfortable the detox will be when you break the habit.

Guess when we learn how to escape difficult thoughts and feelings? In childhood. Here's some examples in my life of how I am seeing this lesson be reinforced:

- When I take my daughters to the doctor to get shots, they get a gummy bear right after the shot.
- I watched my friend's daughter fall and get hurt. She comforted the child with sweets to distract her even though just ten minutes prior she had said she couldn't have a snack because it was almost dinnertime.
- I watched a kid at the playground get to look at pictures and videos on his dad's phone to comfort him after he had gotten upset about something that happened with another kid there.

All of these things add up to: "You need instant gratification to cover up the pain, both physical and emotional, that you are experiencing because you can't really handle it." Reading this, you might be thinking, "But those people were just trying to help!" Of course each had good intentions, but do you see how it subconsciously primes escape addiction?

Our intentions may be totally pure, but we have to think long-term with how we respond to kids who are angry, sad, overwhelmed, or hurting. Teaching them healthy coping skills for pain tolerance and emotional regulation isn't as pretty or fun (or, let's be honest, easy) as giving them colorful gummy bears or a funny dog video. I look back at my life and think that had I been taught healthier ways to face reality, maybe I wouldn't run to TV shows or my phone when things get negative now.

All in all, we need to be more aware of our own escape addictions and how we teach or reinforce it in others. We all can and need to take a break from reality from time to time, but ask yourself: "Is what I am doing helping me or hurting me in the long run?" Go have that night out to let loose but don't make it a habit. Enjoy that TV series but set a time limit for yourself. Buy those special shoes that you have been eyeing for weeks, but make sure you are not then spending on even more things that you don't need. The seductive nature of escape addiction will make it super easy to justify all of these things, but I have found real self-care doesn't need justification. Real self-care actually takes care of you and rarely involves a glass of wine and a bubble bath or staying up late binge watching a series. Real self-care is changing unhealthy habits and learning healthier belief systems. It's facing life with a support system and making your life simpler by decreasing stress you may be adding to your life. It's looking at ways you are attempting to escape uncomfortable and painful thoughts and emotions and reminding yourself you are capable beyond your current belief system to endure what is in front of you.

Key Takeaways

- ✧ Escape addiction sneaks up on us as we slowly escape more and more from the things we do not want to feel. We sometimes call it self-care when in reality it is not.

- ✧ We are taught this form of addiction from early on and need to be aware of how we teach the next generation to handle negative emotions.
- ✧ The longer we fall into escape addiction, the harder it is to pull ourselves out of it and start facing our grief.
- ✧ Real self-care involves us changing negative habits and adjusting false beliefs to healthier ones so we can remember how truly capable we are.

Real Grief Stories

After ten years of marriage I learned that my husband was unhappy and had been for over a year and had not said anything. He wanted time apart to think about it, but truth was he had already made up his mind. I was shocked of course and then angry that he'd been unhappy for so long. I was oscillating between wanting to bargain to make it work. But deep down knowing this was the right thing, to end it. Once the decision was made, I felt a relief. I still toggled through all the stages of grief while the paperwork was being processed and even after. I knew in the end despite the pain and anger, it was for the best.

What is the deeper meaning you have found in your grief?

I was set free. I made a choice out of fear and brainwashing about how life should be but had no idea at the time. This change gave me the freedom to find what I really wanted in life, not live how someone else thought I should be living. I found myself. I found more joy and happiness and explored all sort of things that interested me. The whole marriage wasn't a loss. It brought me to where I was supposed to be and set in motion a slow series of events to bring me to where I am today.

What special or powerful experience led you to find this meaning?

I remember sitting on the floor of my house on a weekend morning in the throes of the divorce with my dogs and thinking how freeing it was to not have to answer to anyone, to get up and do whatever I wanted whenever I wanted. I began to explore other alternatives such as psychics/mediums/energy readers. My exploration of that and spiritualism ultimately lead me to break free of my being somewhat dependent on someone financially and fully realizing I really can do it, and reinventing how I want to live. Finding my interests and digging in and imagining how I want to shift my career to do what I am passionate about, finally truly becoming me.

Angela, 44, Netherlands

CHAPTER 5
BARGAINING: DO WE REALLY HAVE THAT MUCH CONTROL?

I believe the bargaining phase has two sides. One side is before something bad occurs like a death or a loss. If we know it is coming, we bargain with our higher power that if we do or don't do something, then the death or loss will not occur. The other side is after the event has occurred. We play the event over and over in our minds thinking of every possible thing we could have done differently to change the outcome. It's almost like we are trying to change the outcome by replaying the event over and over in our minds and seeking a better resolution. Both phases are about control. Our brains want to believe that we have way more control than we actually do.

Growing up in a religious family, the concept of "earning" the good things that come to me was directly and indirectly communicated. This idea is taught in secular families too. It makes sense because when we are good, we get rewards, but when we are bad, there are consequences. Think about the concept of Santa. If you are good, you get presents, and if you are bad, you get coal. Many religions present a similar idea: If we are good, we please our higher power and good things happen, and if we are bad, we displease our higher power. Several of us were taught this as kids while we were growing up and, sadly, as adults many of us are still stuck in this belief system and hold ourselves and others to this idea as well.

The reality is life happens, positive and negative, and it's not about how good or bad we are. This resolves the whole issue with how good things happen to "bad" people and bad things happen to "good" people. It's because life happens to both...all of life. Plus, something that happens to me I might label as bad and you label as good, so it's truly a subjective experience.

When we are in the bargaining stage, we believe that we can actually control the negative outcome by our actions. Some examples of this phase:

"If I stop drinking and pray every day, then God will you keep my grandmother alive?"

"If I work really hard with extra hours, then can the bank not foreclose on my house?

"If I really invest in creating a life here, then can we not have to move again?"

These "If...then…" statements come from a place of panic. We don't want to lose someone or something, and many of us don't like change. When things don't work out the way we want, we can become angry at our higher power, ourselves, or the universe if we believe something more could have been done. It all goes back to childhood again. Someone was usually to blame when something negative happened and a consequence we didn't like usually followed. My four-year-old tries to bargain so hard when she wants something that has been taken away as a consequence because of her behavior. Our panic and style of bargaining brings us right back into those four-year-old shoes, trying to negotiate to get the outcome we want.

THE OTHER SIDE OF BARGAINING

The other side of the bargaining phase involves us playing through the event over and over, sometimes adding to the trauma we have experienced. We don't intend to hurt ourselves, but continuing to think about what we could have done differently compounds feelings of guilt, anxiety, and depression. Worry and stress also take over, causing insomnia, headaches, digestive and skin issues, and physical pain as our bodies hold on to the weight of the situation.

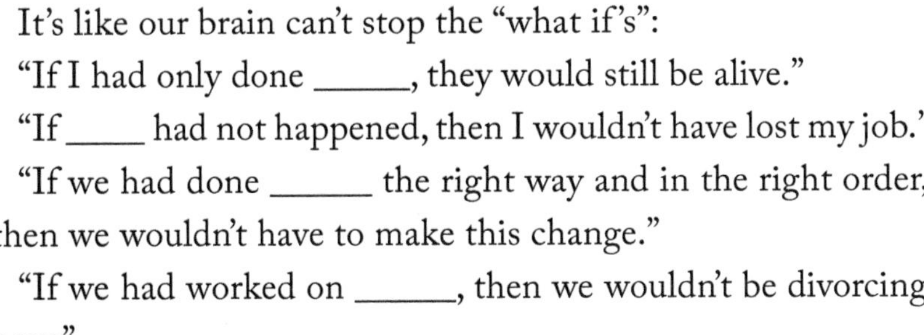

It's like our brain can't stop the "what if's":

"If I had only done _____, they would still be alive."

"If _____ had not happened, then I wouldn't have lost my job."

"If we had done _____ the right way and in the right order, then we wouldn't have to make this change."

"If we had worked on _____, then we wouldn't be divorcing now."

There is a point where we have to let go of control and see that the situation played out the way that it did, even if something you said or did had a direct impact on the negative outcome. You made a choice and cannot change it. You said or did that thing and now you have to live with the consequences. Or the flip side: They said or did that thing and now you have to live with the consequences. Either way acceptance is important to moving through this phase.

We must let go of the belief that we can control everything. Bargaining in this way is just torturing ourselves. Imagine what it would be like if we didn't need to blame anyone for negative events that occur in our lives? Well, we don't have to blame anyone if we don't want to. We actually have a choice in this. In the same way that you made a decision and it affected the outcome of the event, you have a choice now to put an end to your bargaining. If someone else made the decision, then recognize torturing yourself over the outcome and what could have been different doesn't change anything.

Sometimes acceptance is purely releasing the desire to control everything.

The moment we realize this, it frees us and those around us from the challenges bargaining can bring into our lives.

THE BIG R

I was working with a client who was stuck in her grief journey. She was falling into the blame and bargaining game about a friend who had committed suicide. My heart broke for her as session after session she seemed to replay every scenario she could think of where she believed she could have done something differently. In one of our sessions, she began the same process and I stopped her. It was a turning point in her therapy and grief journey.

I asked my client if she had respected her friend when she was living. She said, "Yes, of course." I asked if she had respected choices her friend made in the past even if she didn't agree with them. She thought for a moment and said, "Yes." I then asked her what it would take for her to do the same now and respect her friend's decision to have taken her life even though she didn't agree with that choice. Tears flowed.

See, the bargaining phase makes us believe we have more control than we do in many of life's scenarios, and it negates respect for others and their life plans. What do I mean by this? When we try to bargain to keep someone alive, we are not respecting their life path. When we play "what if" with ourselves over and over, we lose sight of the fact that maybe the outcome is exactly what it was supposed to be. I realize this may tug at some people's belief systems, but ultimately, we all die and no one really knows the exact day, time, or reason. Most of us like to assume it will happen when we are old and gray, and if a death happens before that, there was something wrong. I don't agree with this. I believe we are not all meant to live long lives and that if someone dies earlier than planned, nothing went wrong.

When I was pregnant with my second daughter, we moved to Germany. It was a big international move with our two-year-old, but we knew it would be easier to do before I had our second child. As we got closer to the delivery date, both my husband and I realized we needed some support when it came to delivering in a German hospital. So, we searched for a doula to be there with us during the delivery. A friend had already passed on the name of someone weeks before, and I had kept her information.

The day came for me to meet our potential doula. I was a bit worried she would be the type that I call a rainbows-and-butterflies doula. My first birth had been scary. Birth itself is a beautiful trauma that comes with it a lot of unknowns, and I needed someone realistic by my side. We met, and she told me her story. Not only was Darby not a rainbows-and-butterflies doula, she had been through one of the most difficult experiences I could ever imagine. Sadly, she had lost her son a few days after his estimated due date and gave birth to him knowing he wasn't alive. Darby fully understood that giving birth had no guarantees and was a process that can bring with it a lot of grief.

She shared that she had decided to become a doula after she lost her son. Now she serves other moms who have lost their babies. She works with them in their grief and processing their experiences. I was talking with her one day in my kitchen and shared that I was trying to figure out how to write a chapter on bargaining. I wondered if it even needed to be added in my book. She stopped me and shared how much she still gets stuck in the phase, replaying the days leading up to her son's death and thinking about how she could have changed the outcome. Darby understands that death happens and still faces this phase with a challenge at times. We can all learn from this that it is ok to continue to work on different phases of grief even years later.

I once left a voicemail for Darby as she was preparing for the anniversary of her son's death. I thought really hard about what to say, and something kept tugging at me. Did experiencing the loss of a child have to happen in order for her to become a doula and support so many women through their births and even some through their losses? What if his life, though extremely short, was the catalyst for her growing in such a way that she could sit with women in some of their darkest hours when others could not? In her response, she had shared with me that she had thought about this before too. This is respecting the lifespan a person has. It's realizing that even those who leave this world very quickly can leave a lasting impact.

The loss of a baby is one of the deepest griefs one can experience. My own miscarriages, though different from Darby's experience, cut deep in me, even with two children already. I spent a lot of time playing through the scenarios, but now that I have my third child, I see those miscarriages taught me a lot about life. They helped me understand more about the impermanence of it all, and they helped me work through more of the grief I had around my first birth experience leading me to be more prepared for my third.

Bargaining in grief is trying to take control of the uncontrollable. The moment we start respecting that life needs to happen with positives and negatives, whether we like it or not, is the moment we start to see life and our experiences differently.

- ✧ Bargaining can come in two forms: to keep an event from happening; how we could have changed what happened.
- ✧ Bargaining is our desire to control the uncontrollable.
- ✧ When we begin to respect that life has positive and negative events regardless of who we are, we limit the need for bargaining in our grief process.

Real Grief Stories

The most intense grief I have felt in my life was after the death of my son, Eliot. He died three days after his estimated due date and was born still. His death involved the loss of so many things—the loss of his life, which was limited to the nine months I was pregnant with him; the loss of his smile and seeing his eyes; and the loss of the life experiences I thought we would have together. I have also learned to grieve the loss of the person I was before, since this loss changed me on a very fundamental level.

What is the deeper meaning you found in your grief?

I understood the meaning of my loss only moments after learning my son had died. During my pregnancy with him, I had decided to become a doula and had even read training material about supporting pregnancy losses only a few weeks prior. I knew I could only get through labor if I understood that there was a purpose to the emotional pain of losing him. That purpose was that it helps me understand and support other women through such devastating losses. I also think there is a difference between purpose and meaning. The meaning is more abstract, more spiritual, and shows itself in unexpected, yet wonderful ways, as I support each family while they welcome and sometimes lose their babies.

Darby, 35, Germany

CHAPTER 6

ANGER: THE STORM THAT RAGES INSIDE US

When I think of the anger that comes with grief, a particular friend pops to mind. She wasn't aggressive or outwardly angry. This friend had grief building up inside her after years of losses, changes, adaptations, and rites of passages. You could see it in her eyes. It came out in her tone of voice when certain topics came up in discussions. Her grief was stuck in the phase of anger, and she wasn't sure how to let it out safely.

We talked about her grief one day, and I asked her if I could guide her in a meditation to see what was going on. She closed her eyes, took a deep breath, and we went on a journey to where her mind wanted to take her. My friend felt her grief begin to explode inside her, and she could see the anger as a symbol. She described it as a hurricane, this wind that was blowing so hard. It was like it could knock her down and keep her there. I continued to walk her through the meditation and had her face that wind. I asked her what she would say if she could speak to the wind to see what it would actually do if she addressed it. All the tenseness in her body relaxed. She wasn't speaking yet, but I could tell something was shifting. The energy of anger was finally being acknowledged and sat with.

As she opened her eyes, I asked my friend what she had said to the wind. She shared that she had told the wind that it could blow past her, but it could not destroy her. She explained that after she said this to the wind, it lost all its power and that the wind turned into a gentle breeze that moved around her. It didn't desire to knock her down but did need to be acknowledged. She was able to face it, talk to it, and know that it wasn't the horrible wind she had feared it was. Her windstorm became manageable, and she finally understood it. It wasn't the wind she had feared but the destruction that would come with it. She shared that now she knows she cannot be destroyed, even when it feels like the wind is raging inside her.

Anger can feel like it will take us over. It's an emotion that most of us can say we physically feel before we even know what is making us angry. This hurricane that wants to destroy just needs to be acknowledged and given a healthy outlet. It's not very often, though, that we release anger in ways that don't lead to negative outcomes. Most of us were not taught how to express anger in healthy and appropriate ways. This is why it is so important we work on healthy ways to express emotions so that we model it for the next generations.

CAN YOU ESCAPE THE ANGER?

There is escaping grief like we talked about before with denial and the addiction to escaping, and then there is trying to escape a specific phase of grief. Anger was the phase I, like my friend, got really good at trying to escape, or so I thought. I shared with my husband that I had been trying to escape anger for so long and in doing so rage was building inside me. His response surprised me: "You have been more angry in the past two years than any other time I have known you."

Wait, what? But I thought I had been avoiding anger moving straight into sadness. I thought I had been doing such a good job of escaping it that no one could see it. Nope. By trying to do this, I had shifted into being more irritable, angry, and at times exploding at silly things because I couldn't contain it anymore. Sometimes when we think we are avoiding or escaping a phase of grief, it's actually oozing out of our pores and everyone else can see it. It's like eating garlic and later hoping no one notices. Believe me, they all notice!

If I am completely honest, anger is my least favorite emotion. It feels like a huge wildfire inside of me that will not be able to be contained if I finally let it out. Many of my female clients have shared the same struggle. Anger is such a healthy emotion, but it has taken me a long time personally to come to this realization so that I could help others express it in positive ways. I think our society gets anger all wrong though, especially for women.

As a woman, when I get angry, I'm being "emotional, crazy, a bitch, mean, stepping out of line, (insert any other judgmental keep-you-in-a-box comment you can think of)." When men get angry, they are "unsafe, reactive, have issues" and those judgments for both genders need to disappear. Anger is an expression of something not aligning inside of us. A line has been crossed. A hurt uncovered. A rightful emotion for us to have. However, it is how we act in our anger that has led to so many negative connotations. Let's be honest, some of us can react in such horrible, reactive ways that can cause short-term and long-term problems, which then cause anger in our lives to be scary.

THE WILDFIRE

Let's look at anger as a wildfire. Fire causes destruction, death, pain, but it can also be necessary for regrowth. The vision of a phoenix rising from the ashes wouldn't exist without the fire. As one of the elements of the earth, it is needed and part of the ecosystem. So, this fire inside of us is necessary. It is part of our emotional system that will show up when we need to destroy (change or let go of something) and/or create something.

WHAT ANGER MIGHT NEED TO DESTROY:

- ✧ False beliefs we have or that others have that we have taken on
- ✧ Feelings of tension and pain (hence why it feels good to work out when angry)
- ✧ Beliefs that we could have saved something from happening
- ✧ Inequalities and injustices

WHAT ANGER MIGHT NEED TO CREATE:

- ✧ Beauty through art, music, writing, and expression
- ✧ New neural pathways to reroute old patterns of thinking

- ✧ A new you developed from hitting rock bottom
- ✧ A movement or empowerment of others to create a greater change

My journey of grief clearly couldn't skip this part no matter what I did. It was showing up despite how much I believed I was not letting it out. Maybe you have found yourself in this same situation? You think you don't "need" to feel a particular emotion in your grief because _____ (enter any excuse that we try to convince ourselves of), but without you realizing it, it's showing up.

It's been my experience working with clients and going through the phase of anger myself that once you give yourself permission to just see what's there in regards to your emotions around grief, the emotions are not as scary as you may have thought they would be. Another way to look at anger in grief is as the monster under our bed that's actually just a teddy bear waiting to be held. We won't know till we look. Most of the time though we stay hidden under our covers hoping it'll just go away on its own.

I believed that when I finally let out my anger about everything I had experienced in life, that it would never stop coming out of me. A dam being released and unable to be closed up again. I thought that it was so powerful that I wouldn't be able to contain it. I believed this so strongly that anger became a monster inside of me instead of what it really was. Anger comes with an energy that wants to move. It can destroy and create, and it communicates its needs to us. We have to listen though. I had focused so long on the destructive side of anger that I thought that's all it was. I was wrong.

In the beginning of 2020, it was time to slowly release some pressure from the soda bottle of anger that had been shaking vigorously inside of me. For years I had used this example with clients, and it was time to recognize it as a real analogy of anger in my own life. I wasn't sure what would come as I started to do the healing work needed, but after the conversation with my husband about my anger, I knew I needed to do something. I took some time to reflect in a journal after I spent a morning letting my anger express itself:

> *Anger has been the phase of grief I have skipped over for the last eighteen months since Mom died. When it comes up, I have received messages from others that something is wrong with me if I have all this anger inside me. Logically, as a therapist, I know this isn't true, but as a woman with her own past, I began to believe I had to contain the fire inside me. It started to turn into rage and showed up at different times.*
>
> *Today, I realized I have to start letting the air out of the soda bottle I keep shaking up. If I open it up all the way, it will look like rage and impact others. If I slowly open the cap a little at a time but with purpose and on a regular basis (which I have not been doing), then it doesn't hurt the ones I love and I get the release I need.*
>
> *I wanted to create with my anger, not destroy. So I remembered several years ago learning from an*

art therapist about anger art. I ran inside, grabbed a red marker, and several sheets of paper. I started writing all over the papers everything that made me angry in life. Everything.

Each page I finished I ripped up into little pieces. I knew I was done when I started to begin the next sentence and then my mind went blank. I had hit on what I needed. Now for the art.

I got a huge piece of paper and glue. I knew immediately I wanted to create a butterfly. Each small piece of paper with bright red writing on it started to form the wings of the butterfly like a mosaic. And so my art was created. My anger has beauty in it. I will hang it up with pride. I know there is more release to come, and I know I have several options on how. I am no longer afraid my anger will engulf me. It's a part of me that wants to speak too, and now I am giving it a voice.

My anger didn't want to destroy. In fact, I felt worse when I tried to release it that way. When I listened to it, I finally heard what it needed to do: to create. If we think about it, anger has created some wonderful changes in our world. We just tend to label them differently. It has inspired some of the greatest visionaries and artists for centuries. It has led to huge movements by people young and old. Think of women getting the right to vote, the AMBER Alert being created, domestic violence organizations forming, and the Black Lives Matter movement. Anger has created unity in groups as they come together to make change, even if that change isn't something everyone else agrees with.

Let's address the destructive side of anger. Anger also wants to destroy, and this cannot be escaped from either. It wants others to see and hear the pain that's going on inside. See, I would just skip to the part where I tell people about the pain and sadness. I thought it was an easy pass on what might come out if I let it start as anger. This is a phase that has to be acknowledged and listened to or it will make itself known in other ways. This can be how our anger leads us to hurt others and ourselves. Finding healthy ways to express anger when it says it wants to destroy is crucial.

Some choose to go for runs, work out, throw things away, rip up papers, break items (that are not important...hopefully), box with a sofa or bed, visit a rage room, rap, yell in their car, scream into a pillow...the possibilities are endless. You must find what works for you and is safe. I watched a documentary once where a woman brought a bucket of rocks up a small hill and threw the rocks down as she shouted out what she was angry about. It helped her feel so much better and caused no actual destruction.

I once experienced so much anger that I called my brother (he was the only one who answered after I called several friends), promised him everything was ok but to pull the phone away from his ear so I could get something out, and then I yelled with all my might. I kept yelling until it was all out. I wanted my anger to be heard without hurting anyone.

My poor brother wasn't quite sure if I was really ok, but once I explained that I needed to let my anger out and for someone to hear it but for it not to hurt anyone (like cursing someone out, calling them names, or saying things that lead me to be physically reactive) he understood. We've all been there. It's needed, too. Our anger wants a witness. It helps validate for us that it is safe and accepted.

Key Takeaways

- ✧ Anger can be a scary emotion, but once we face it and understand what it is telling us, we are able to heal.
- ✧ Society makes anger a negative emotion that shouldn't be shown making it harder to express it in socially appropriate and effective ways.
- ✧ Anger can destroy and create. Both can be healthy.
- ✧ By listening to ourselves and our needs in a quiet moment, we can identify what our anger needs to do to be released.

Real Grief Stories

Leading up to my eighth birthday, my father passed away, leaving my twelve-year-old sister, me, and my mom. All three of us experienced his passing differently, and we all moved on with our lives differently. As I was so young, I didn't have many memories of my father. When I started growing up, I began to see an absence in my life. Along with this absence, and teenage angst, I started to feel a constant glooming sadness over my being. I had never felt connected to my father, nor did I have a current father figure, and I began to search for ways that he and I were similar. In the beginning, I rarely found anything that rooted us together, and I began to feel estranged and angry toward him. As I grew more into the person I am today, I found unique mannerisms or hobbies about my father that I inherently do as well.

What is the deeper meaning you have found in your grief?

I think I was lucky enough to find two different meanings in my grief. I learned that the more I focused on who I was and was going to be, the more my father came out. Maybe this is because he was my parent and whether I look like him or not, I will always have parts of him inside me. The more I follow my own ambitions and beliefs, the more I hear my father in my head encouraging me and I can feel him believing in me. The other meaning I found was that the person you have lost cannot be replaced; but those who try and fill that void with love and compassion are a wonderful stand-in. I grew up without a father, but I have father figures in my life that have taught me lessons and supported me unconditionally, just like a real father would.

Samantha, 21, Brazil

CHAPTER 7

DEPRESSION AND SADNESS: THE HOLE WE CIRCLE...UNTIL WE FALL IN

When I walk into a room, I am a sponge to people's emotions, especially sadness. When I sense or see someone sad, I feel this drop inside me and I get quiet and present with them. I can safely say that sadness and I are well acquainted with each other. You might describe me as empathic. Ok, you would definitely describe me as empathic. Even at a young age, I could sense when someone was hurting and would go and sit with them. As I got older, I noticed that I experienced my emotions on a deeper level too.

Depression showed itself in my life in my teen years after my parents' divorce and continued to pop up throughout young adulthood. Medication helped at times, but my sadness and depression showed up regularly because of my grief. When I started doing the work in my mid-twenties to address all of my grief, I found medicine was no longer needed. That's not everyone's journey, please know this. For me, though, it was the key to my mental health improving. I just had to face years' worth of grief, and it was not easy.

After my mom died, someone shared with me a powerful quote by Edna St. Vincent Millay. She said: "Where you used to be, there is a hole in the world, which I find myself constantly walking around in the daytime, and falling in at night." I find that nights are the hardest when I am in the phase of grief called depression or sadness. It's like I have tried all day to maintain and manage, and when night hits, I fall into the hole. Do you know this feeling too?

Depression and sadness show themselves in a variety of ways. You may be tearful on a regular basis, lose interest in things that you once loved, pull away from people you normally hang out with, quit activities that you regularly participated in, struggle to get out of bed, shower, and complete basic hygiene daily. Thoughts can be described as empty or overwhelming. My clients share they tend to focus mainly on the negative things that have happened to them. They feel like a dark cloud is constantly over them and like they cannot think or see clearly. Many say they feel like they have given up trying and are doing the bare minimum to "get by" each day.

Most clients I see who are dealing with grief come to me in this phase or at the point of burnout from trying to escape it for so long. I can see it in their eyes. Grief has a look to it that peers through the eyes to see if it's safe to come out. Almost like it's asking, "Can you handle the level of emotion I am about to release?" This is the stage where people start apologizing the most, like crying is something to be sorry for.

Let's take a moment to think about this. Why do we think

we need to apologize for crying or letting out our emotions? I don't care how ugly your crying face is, you are allowed to let it out without apologizing! I can totally understand warning someone that you are about to cry (if you can), but I think the more of us that unapologetically cry when we need to will help future generations be more comfortable with difficult emotions. I asked women from a multitude of cultures, countries, and backgrounds about apologizing when crying. A majority of them said they do apologize. They shared they were worried they were a burden on others, that it would make the other person uncomfortable, or that it makes them feel weak, leading them to apologize.

Now think about this: How often in your life have you felt like it was a burden for someone you cared about to cry in front of you? Yes, you may have been uncomfortable because you were not quite sure what to say, but I bet you wouldn't tell them to stop. You would tell them you were there for them and wanted to help but didn't know how to. Do you see the person you love who is crying in front of you as weak? Probably not. Wouldn't it be nice if we held ourselves to the same expectations we hold others to?

> The faster we start to allow ourselves to be emotional in front of those we trust without apologizing, the more we will heal.

THE POWER OF UGLY CRYING

Sadness and tears are our bodies' natural expression. When we try to stuff them down and not experience them, we can really hurt ourselves. Stress headaches, stomach issues, and panic attacks can all come from holding in sadness and not allowing ourselves to cry. We put a lot of effort into avoiding crying though! Imagine if we put all that effort into actually doing something healthy for ourselves. Well, this would mean we would need to allow ourselves to cry, which puts us right back to what feels uncomfortable again.

Some of you may read this and know that you are actually quite comfortable with crying. Thank you! Please teach the rest of us that this is perfectly normal and healthy. Tears are our bodies' natural release of tension. Crying is good and powerful. Not to mention healthy!

You know when you finally do let yourself cry and it gets to the point where you have to breathe through your mouth because you have cried so hard and so much? Your nose is like a dripping faucet and you've soaked through a whole box of tissues. Do you remember the feeling afterwards? When you finally take that deep breath of release. It's like a huge sigh. Your body can't release any more tears and you feel a sense of peace. You may still feel sadness, but the release that was needed has finally happened. This. This is where crying is powerful. It creates a healing that words can't.

I find that most of the grieving process needs to occur without words. It needs to be felt and expressed accordingly. The sadness and mourning that comes with grief is just as essential as any other phase, but it's where the most healing occurs. So ugly cry it all out and take those deep healing breaths. You need the release.

I DON'T WANT TO GET OUT OF BED

Let's address the parts of depression that can hit the hardest. We will experience times in our depression and sadness where we don't want to get out of bed and don't want to brush our teeth or shower. We let our house become chaos and eat all the Chinese takeout we can (or whatever your favorite takeout food is). We begin to isolate ourselves. This can be a slippery slope. This is the part of grief that scares a lot of people. When we are used to being active and wanting to do things and then all of a sudden we lose all interest. Also, I have come to realize it's scary because many of us watched family members do this and seem to lose themselves.

Let me remind you that often what we saw growing up were unhealthy ways of grieving. I shared before that this is the phase where most clients come to me for help. There is a reason why. This is one of the phases where we need support the most. We need accountability to create simple, healthy habits and not be made to feel guilty if we can't keep up. We often need a safe space to talk about what is making us sad and depressed, and this can mean saying things we might be afraid to say to people we love. You may not be interested in therapy, but even a coach, spiritual leader, guide, or healer are excellent supporters when we need the help. I will note that not every counselor or supporter is the right person for you, so understand you may need to see a couple different people to find the right fit for you. The beauty is that during this day and age most of these supporters can do online sessions, so you don't have to leave your bed...at least not at first.

What I have learned from sadness is that it doesn't have to swallow up weeks or months of my life. It may just take up a day or two, or even just an hour or so depending on what it is related to. The less I run from it or try to distract myself, the easier it is to go through this phase. This is the phase most associated with the term "grieving." It's the tears, the heartbreak, and the missing of what is no longer here. Sadness is a powerful part of the letting go process and can't be rushed. I equate this phase to the shedding of the old skin to welcome the fresh new you. We must shed all of the "before" version of ourselves to fully transform into a more empowered version of ourselves.

Key Takeaways

- Most people come to therapy when they are in the depths of the sadness phase of grief.
- You don't need to apologize for crying. It's a normal expression of emotion, and it is part of the healing process.
- Seeking support when you are struggling to get out of bed can help you during this phase of grief.

Real Grief Stories

My best friend was diagnosed with breast cancer at the age of thirty, six months after her mom passed away from breast cancer. She went through surgery and chemo for a year and she was clean. Nine months after that, the cancer came back and spread everywhere. I knew she had no time left, but I denied it for months. She passed away at the age of thirty-three, and I did everything but accept the reality. A year after she passed I quit my job due to anxiety and panic attacks. I started therapy and slowly I experienced grief. I was in denial for a year believing time would pass and it would get better. I had no idea.

What is the deeper meaning you have found in your grief?

I realized how much I love life and how lucky I was to be alive and experience it.

What special or powerful experience led you to find this meaning?

I was asking myself constantly what's the point of life and being alive if we don't know what's coming next and how unfair life is. After I left my job I had plenty of time. I went to the river on my own that summer quite often and I preferred the mornings without too many people around. A young woman with her young daughter and their dog sat down on the other side of the river. The mom was putting sun cream on her kid, and she went to the water and started playing with their dog and somehow in that moment I thought THIS is the purpose of life. Experiencing these small moments.

Neda, 39, Germany

CHAPTER 8
ACCEPTANCE: LETTING THE WOUND HEAL

I remember watching *The Avengers* in the first year after my mom's death. There is a moment in the film during a big battle when Captain America says to Bruce Banner that he needs to get angry so he can become the Hulk. Bruce responds that his secret is, he is always angry.

It was then that I realized when someone said I seemed to be doing well, I wanted to correct them:

"You seem like you are doing so well after your mom's death."

"Well, my secret is, I'm always grieving."

Isn't that the truth? It doesn't disappear. It's always there. The more you accept this, the less energy you waste fighting it. Acceptance doesn't mean accepting the loss or change immediately. This will come with time. Acceptance means realizing that you are grieving because there is a loss that cannot be filled by anyone or anything else. When we moved throughout my childhood, I see now that I didn't need to accept we were moving again. I needed to accept that I was grieving each time. Now as a kid, this isn't a concept I was going to understand, but I see now how I can teach this to my children when change occurs that they do not like.

When we moved to Germany, my husband experienced reverse culture shock. This happens when a person returns to their home country after living abroad and no longer feels like they belong to that culture like they did before. Living in the USA for over five years had change my husband and there was no going back. It took him a long time to accept the new lens he saw his country of origin through. When he realized he was grieving though, he was able to accept that it was going to be hard and an adjustment. There was no need to rush the process, but his understanding of what was going on relieved the feelings of anger and frustration he experienced as he navigated his home country in a new way.

ACCEPTING AND FORGIVING

Acceptance and forgiveness tend to go hand in hand. Depending on what type of loss or life challenge you have faced or are facing, you may be looking at both at the same time in your grief journey. Let's address the truths about them. Both acceptance and forgiveness are powerful tools to help you heal, but they tend to lead people to think that they must be "ok" with what was done to them or what they experienced. The truths about acceptance and forgiveness are that you do not have to like what happened, you do not have to agree with what happened, and you certainly do not have to continue a relationship with anyone who was a part of the reason you needed to grieve.

For example, someone who is in an abusive relationship and is eventually able to get out of it will need to do grief work. As they do the work, they will come to a point where they realize forgiveness is needed. Now the playground method of forgiving is to forgive and keep playing with the kid. The adult process, though, is to forgive and learn. Learning sometimes means we separate ourselves and keep a boundary from a person or thing that negatively affects us. Learning can also mean giving another chance but with limits, in less severe cases of course.

The key to acceptance and forgiveness is releasing yourself from the continual pain of holding on to something that no longer serves you. Think of a deep cut on your hand. If you don't clean it and just put a bandage on it, it probably will get infected and become a more serious and critical problem for you. If you clean it and treat it with the medicines it needs, bandage it up, and continue to take good care of it, it will heal much faster and more easily.

Forgiveness and acceptance are like this. We work on treating the wound not by pounding more dirt and germs into it but by cleaning out the old. This can be painful, which is a large reason why people avoid working on their grief. Once we do the difficult work, then we treat it with "medicine" and a "bandage." In this case, it's support and help. We allow it to heal and give it the time it needs. This may also mean limiting how much we use our hand or changing up how we work. All a part of our mental and emotional healing process as well. For someone working on their grief this means adapting the way they do things to allow for grieving and full healing. In the end, we release behaviors and habits that continue to hurt us and take the time to allow grief to integrate into who we are now.

I accept that my mom died. It makes me sad, but I don't ache every day like I used to. It doesn't mean I am happy with what happened. I just accept that it occurred and history cannot be re-written, so no need for bargaining. I also accept and respect that it was her time to go. It took me a long time and a lot of work to get to this point, but I realized by believing otherwise I was throwing dirt in my wound. This realization came after I dove headfirst into my grief journey and did the work to accept and forgive. When we continue to believe that a story could have gone differently, we stay stuck in the past instead of accepting how the story actually happened and moving forward into our future.

Forgiveness puts the power back in your hands, as does acceptance. It says "I choose to no longer let this impact me in negative ways." It doesn't mean roll over. It means learn and grow. Know your truth and what you need. Stand firm in your boundaries and understand your choices better. No longer allow yourself to be the victim to your circumstances. Forgiveness gives you the control so you can be more present and live your life.

IT'S NOT GOING TO BE EASY

Let me be clear, both acceptance and forgiveness are challenging in their own way and take time. They also both have to occur in order for you to move forward. There was a lot of forgiveness work I needed to do around my mom's death, and funnily enough some of it was with God. If you are spiritual, you might laugh at this, or you may totally get where I am coming from. I needed to forgive God for how my mom died so suddenly and how she was no longer in our lives. Was it God I really needed to forgive? No, as is the case so often with grief, we like to place the blame on someone or something. My beef was with God, and so forgiveness work was important.

What I realized, though, was that I needed to have some long meetings with myself in front of the mirror. Why did I believe that my mom should live to a certain age? Did someone guarantee that for me? Or did I just assume that because that's what I wanted? My forgiveness work actually led me to change my thinking about how life events *actually* work and how I get in the way with my expectations of how life *should* go. I know better than anyone else to stop *shoulding* on myself, but sometimes I can't help it. I started changing my "why me?" thinking into "why not me?" thinking.

Life is going to happen to all of us. Learning how to accept and forgive are powerful tools to have in our toolbox. A lot of the time, what we really need to do is face ourselves and start our forgiveness and acceptance work within. This is not easy. Pride gets in the way, defensiveness kicks in, and we want to blame everyone and everything else. Let me fill you in on a little secret: it's ok to not be perfect and to make mistakes. It's ok that you can't rescue or heal everyone. It's ok that you will say and do things that you wish you could take back. I believe part of life is learning these lessons, which is why forgiving ourselves and accepting our humanity are important in our grief process.

Key Takeaways

- ✧ Acceptance and forgiveness are core healing steps of grief.
- ✧ Forgiving doesn't mean not learning from the event. On the contrary, forgiveness means releasing yourself from the bitterness and anger of what happened and growing from it with better boundaries and experience.
- ✧ Forgiveness and acceptance are like finally cleaning out a wound that has become infected. It doesn't always feel good, but it is crucial to complete healing.
- ✧ Many times we need to start with ourselves when working in the phases of forgiveness and acceptance before forgiving others.

Real Grief Stories

When I was twenty, I lost my boyfriend to leukemia. He broke up with me before his death, saying we wouldn't have stayed together anyway. I wanted to travel the world; he wanted to live a quiet life. His parents, in their own grief, saw this as a means to bully me and kick me out of his life. When he died three months later, it was a shock because I didn't have time to talk to him for one last time. Adding to this situation, my mother had cancer two years before that and blamed me for it, repeatedly. It was the culmination of years of psychological violence from her. This new event made this older wound so much deeper.

What is the deeper meaning you have found in your grief?

This situation as a whole pushed me to finally find the courage to realize my dreams. I always wanted to travel. Four years before, I had a short but passionate relationship with a boy who did a student exchange in my hometown. We had kept in touch but not spoken directly apart from the occasional email. So we got in touch on chat, and planned a trip around Europe together. This event led me back to him, and we have been together eleven years since. If I hadn't been through my problems with my mom, and the death of my ex-boyfriend, I don't think I would have found the courage to do what I did. After all this, it appeared clear to me that it was the one thing to do. I couldn't accept more shit in my life, and I couldn't be controlled by anyone anymore.

Stephanie, 33, Germany

CHAPTER 9

FINDING MEANING IN IT ALL

The last and most recently identified phase of grief is called finding meaning. David Kessler wrote the book *Finding Meaning: The Sixth Stage of Grief* in 2019 explaining this phase, and I couldn't be happier. Let me first catch you up on who David is. He is a famous grief expert, speaker, and author. David co-authored two books with Dr. Elisabeth Kübler-Ross (who founded the original five stages of grief in 1969...more on her later). Both of those books, *Life Lessons: Two Experts on Death and Dying Teach Us About the Mysteries of Life and Living* and *On Grief and Grieving: Finding the Meaning of Grief Through the Five Stages of Loss* he wrote with Dr. Kübler-Ross as she was dying which led to some amazing revelations.

He continues on in Dr. Kübler-Ross's footsteps in educating mental health and healthcare providers about grief. If you get a chance to read about his life, you will be amazed at what he has been through and also see why his life experiences guided him to being an expert on grief. Let's just say he clearly found his meaning in his grief experiences. Now, back to his book. Many of us in the mental health field squished finding meaning in with the acceptance phase, but in reality, they are very different. You can accept what occurred in your life, but not be able to see the meaning of why it happened. Grouping these two together didn't make sense. David explains that not everyone finds meaning in their grief, but those who do, grow in beautiful ways because they see life differently. Those who find meaning in grief tend to see that everything has a purpose whether it makes sense to them in the moment or not. It's taking a more spiritual lens to the process of grief.

HOW DOES ONE FIND MEANING?

I found meaning in my mom's death rather quickly. As I shared my grief process openly online, others wrote to me privately about how it was freeing them to finally go through their own grief journey after years of holding it in. I was inspiring others, and it gave me purpose. Finding a deeper meaning in your life experiences is what helps you find hope and purpose. It removes the victim mentality. Some in my online community have found meanings such as:

"It helped me love people even more deeply."

"It helped me appreciate what I have."

"It was the catalyst to my no longer living in fear and trying something new."

"It helped me see my purpose in life."

"I stopped letting fear take over my life and began enjoying each day!"

"I began an organization to educate others on a cause that was important to me and my family member."

The meanings can feel small or big (though truly they are all the same size!), but finding meaning is beneficial to your healing process. So how does one find meaning in the challenges they face? In grief healing sessions, I always have the client look at what they learned from a particular experience both good and bad. I have them address how it has impacted how they respond to life right now. Typically, it's impacted them negatively because they are stuck in the fear and trauma of the event. Once we heal this, they see the greater meaning and the messages about themselves and about life that give them hope and purpose.

Here's an example of how to do this:

Take a moment and think about something that has caused you grief in your life. Ask yourself,

What deeper lessons did I learn from this experience?

Your answer may include learning things like being more independent, better boundaries with others, how to say goodbye even when it hurts, how to be open to meeting new people, how to trust yourself more than others, recognizing your own strength, seeing the good in people again, seeing that not everyone is a safe person, how to rise above negativity, or being open to trying something new. The answer may come to you quickly or take some time, especially if the pain is really deep. Don't force an answer though.

I have worked with adults on addressing grief from their childhoods, and it can take time to really understand what they learned from the experiences they have gone through. We don't often think about pain and challenges from our childhood in the context of what was learned. One client shared with me about her experience of starting at a new school after moving. She remembered vividly crying on the bus the first day of school and at times still felt stuck in that anxious state when new things happened in her life.

I asked her to close her eyes and sit with that little girl on the bus in her mind. Through a guided meditation, she started to share that from that event on the bus she learned how to take care of herself and that she was capable of handling uncomfortable situations. Though she felt stuck as that little girl on the bus during new situations as an adult, when she shifted her mind into what positive came out of this sad situation she took back control and found meaning in it. She realized that she has always been able to handle new situations even if she feels uncomfortable. Her inner strength was finally acknowledged again.

Once you think of what you learned from a situation, look at how you then applied it or will apply it to your life. The trauma I experienced during my first daughter's birth gave me more of a voice the next time I was about to be in an OR room after our first miscarriage. I was able to ask for what I needed. There is even greater meaning in why her birth was so challenging, but this is one seed that was planted and grew from a very scary situation.

The other meaning I have found from that time was linked to me being unable to get out of the hospital bed for three days. My husband bonded with our daughter in ways he may never have if I had been doing everything after her birth. He changed her diapers and clothes, went to all her checks with the pediatrician in the hospital, and sang to her to soothe her when she was crying. My husband became the dad he was meant to be and desired to be because of our situation. As scary and difficult as that birth experience was, seeing him grow overnight into an amazing father gives such great meaning and purpose to what I went through. Did you notice that from my challenging experience a deeper meaning for someone else, my husband in this situation, came about? Sometimes we can also find the meaning for others in the challenges we face.

NO FAST TRACK IN GRIEF

Very often, people want to jump ahead to finding meaning in why things have happened to them. Some do find it quickly, but if they ignore the process, grief can stay stuck. A marriage may end and open the door for a healthier and better relationship, but if you don't grieve the ending of the first marriage, it will impact the new relationship. Losing a job may open up space for your dream job, but you must look at the loss of the job and how it impacted you. That impact, which sometimes shows up as fear and paranoia about losing another job, may creep up in the new job. Sometimes it just takes a couple of days or weeks to do the work and heal if the grief feels small, and other times it can take months or even years because of the depth.

What I didn't realize at the time right after my mom died was that even if you jump ahead to finding the meaning in your grief, you still have to experience *all* of the grief. There is no golden ticket to jump to the front of the line when it comes to grief, unfortunately! I had hoped that I could skip the painful part. I couldn't. What did help though was during the darkest moments in my grief I was able to see the meaning and purpose as a light at the end of the tunnel.

I always come back to the quote by Thich Nhat Hanh: "No mud, no lotus." To grow into a beautiful flower, we must grow in the mud. We must go through the dark, difficult times. It cannot be rushed. And honestly, once you see the outcome, you may not want it to be. Our instant gratification based society programs us to struggle with anything that takes time, but the reality is healing needs exactly that. Time and attention.

Think about a plant for a second. We put a seed in soil, give it water, and put it somewhere where it can get sunlight. Then what do we do? Continue to water it as needed. We know that in order for the seed to grow and become the plant it was meant to be, it takes time. We don't get angry at the seed for taking too long. We don't get impatient with it. We don't tell it how it should or shouldn't grow. We understand since the age we were taught how seeds work that it takes time for a plant to grow. So we plant the seed, tend to it, and wait. Are we not as important as that seed? Does our healing and care really need to be rushed? Or can it be as we see in nature with anything that grows? Time and attention are key. Relax into the process and it's much easier. I find that by doing this, the ability to find meaning and purpose in our challenges easily becomes clear.

PLAY IT ALL OUT TO THE END

In David Kessler's book *Finding Meaning*, he shares that it would be great if events in our lives were like online solitaire games. We get a notification that no more moves can be made to win, so it's time to move on. It's a reminder that not everything that happens in our lives is meant to work out no matter how we play the game. I believe that many of us intuitively get those messages that say "it's time to move on" or "this isn't going to work out" when it comes to life challenges. The problem is that we get emotionally attached and stay in a hopeful state that it will all work out the way we think it should. Some of the best scenarios that have happened in my life have been one hundred percent opposite of how I believed my life should work out. (Thank goodness for that!) I found the meaning in them after I let go of how I wanted things to occur.

After the birth experience with my daughter, I didn't fully understand the purpose or meaning in why things had to happen the way they did. Why a seemingly normal pregnancy turned negative so fast, leaving me afraid for my life. I knew that afterward I was more grateful to live life and enjoyed things around me on a different level. I was thankful for this newfound meaning, but it wasn't until my first miscarriage that I realized the full effect of what I had learned from the birth experience. I learned to have a voice, especially with medical professionals. I learned how to ask questions and stand up for what I want and need. I learned how to be ok freaking out and emotional about the outcome instead of sucking it up and acting like everything was ok. I learned to be authentic and ask for help. These are some huge nuggets of meaning for me, I must say!

Another tool I teach my clients is to think of their lives like a movie. You get to see why a person goes through the challenges they face. You understand why things didn't work out or why relationships needed to end. You get to see what greater meaning was found from the losses they experienced. Our lives are similar. Look back to when you were younger and faced a challenge, the ending of something, or the loss of someone. Think about what was happening in your life months before. Then think about what happened during and right after the challenge. Look at life now and how that life challenge shaped you, how it impacted how you live your life. There was a greater meaning to why it occurred, and I bet, in hindsight, you have a clearer picture of it all.

Some meaning and purpose shows up later on, when the movie has played out more. Even more meaning will come if my daughters decide to have kids too. I will be able to share what I learned and empower them to seek support and have a voice. I believe that no experience happens without a purpose for someone somewhere. There is always a bigger picture, even if we can't see it in the moment. Lessons can be learned, even if it takes years to figure it out. So, don't give up hope if you haven't found meaning or purpose in your life challenges. Work on healing the deeper roots of pain that may still exist and then see what comes.

Let me share with you an unusual relationship in nature where the greater purpose isn't what you would expect. Fires have long been used to destroy nature in order to create healthier growth on land. My husband and I traveled to Australia years ago on an adventure with our oldest when she was still a baby. We soaked in Australia's culture and went to the local museums to learn about the history of this beautiful country. We learned about the Aboriginals burning parts of the land, they call it fire-stick farming, to encourage new plant growth and bring in more animals for hunting. They strategically removed the old to bring in the new and understood this to be a healthy routine.

Did you know there are even seeds that only sprout after being exposed to fire, like the seeds of the eucalyptus tree? The seeds are housed in a cone or fruit that is closed off with resin. Fire helps to melt that resin away allowing the seed to be released. These trees have adapted over time and actually have properties that encourage fire. It's like they have embraced a part of life that happens in Australia. The fire now serves a purpose for this tree as well as many other trees and plants that need fire to release their seeds into the earth.

Without the loss of the old, the new growth would not occur. Without experiencing the losses and challenges we would not grow in the ways we need to. We must go through the fires of our own grief. What if we could see how much positive comes out of the fires we face before we walked through them? We would definitely approach life challenges differently. Probably with less fear and more faith!

I want to add a little more information for those of you who find a greater "calling" or find their meaning by creating an organization, becoming a speaker or writer, or founding something that takes time and effort. When you do find meaning in your grief, you won't feel motivated every day. Even now, it's clear to me that I am a transformative grief guide, and I also provide others with inspiration on facing life's challenges. However, I have days and weeks where I need to grieve, focus on me and my family, and keep to myself. I want to save my energy for my own process, which is a healthy boundary and extremely important. Again, grief and our process is up to us, not how society thinks it should go. So don't feel like you need to have your switch turned in the on position all the time. That's exhausting, will lead to burn out, and is definitely not part of the meaning of your grief and life challenges. Embrace the meaning you have found in creating something bigger than you and trust in the process as you work on yourself as well.

Key Takeaways

- Finding meaning is the most recent phase of grief, identified by David Kessler, which occurs when you understand the greater purpose in why things have occurred in your life.
- Reflecting on what you have learned from an experience and how it has impacted how you live your life can help you find your meaning.
- Meaning can be "big" or "small" to you but is still just as impactful.
- Life is like a movie that we don't know the ending to yet, so some meaning and purpose from our life challenges can come later on. Don't force yourself to come up with something now if it doesn't come naturally.

PART 3

THE FULL EXPERIENCE OF GRIEF

"Should you shield the valleys from the windstorms,
you would never see the beauty of their canyons."
Dr. Elizabeth Kübler-Ross

I always found the phases of grief to be powerful in helping guide us along a more structured path. Dr. Kübler-Ross originally created the phases or stages of grief for those with terminal illnesses. It was the stages they experienced toward accepting that they were dying. The stages then began to be used by psychologists, psychiatrists, social workers, and counselors for the family members of the person with a terminal illness as well. Later, the stages of grief were used to address grief in all forms as they do a wonderful job of explaining what so many of us go through. They are not sequential stages as we would traditionally think. We can experience a variety of the stages in one day actually. Anger may lead to feelings of sadness and depression. Then our brain kicks into bargaining again, and finally we take a deep breath and just accept that things are the way they are. Remember, though, that the phases are not linear and grief is a process. You may reach a state of acceptance one day and feel emotions from another phase another day. Experiencing acceptance about what happened is a process. I see it as occurring in stages, so do not be surprised if you find new levels of acceptance over time.

The phases or stages of grief are able to normalize our experiences in grief. There are also, however, experiences that can occur in one or multiple phases of grief that should be addressed. When you ask a group of people about their grief experiences, you start to see particular patterns in what is experienced:

- The physical experiences of grief
- The loneliness
- The experience of humor to cope
- The complexity of emotions on special days
- The struggle with how others respond to our grief and how we respond to others who are grieving
- The challenge of feeling shame or embarrassment for how we grieve
- The beauty of experiencing what I call AND emotions that others sometimes shame us for

The following chapters will address each of these concepts and experiences, as I believe they hold importance in our grief journey. They may normalize specifically what you have experienced or are experiencing and help you see the deeper meaning. The phases of grief hold beautiful significance to each of our experiences. Now let's go a step further and learn what occurs within the phases that create a fuller experience of grief.

CHAPTER 10

THE PANIC, PAIN, AND LONGING IN GRIEF

Experiencing the physiological response of grief is the first part of going through the fire, and it is a *must*. It can involve physical pain, a breaking of the heart, difficulty breathing, and the emotion of shock that makes many of us drop to our knees or lose feeling in our limbs. I wish I could tell you there was a way to avoid this part, but there isn't. Just writing this leads me to remember the times I have felt the physical pain of a loss. It's tough on our bodies, but I have come to understand that the more we are willing to go through the phases of grief without a fight, without denial, the more those physical effects of grief are short-lived. We must feel this part of grief to know we can move forward through any obstacle that comes our way. It may not feel this way, but you will come out of it on the other side.

THE PANIC

I must have been seven or eight years old. My younger brother and I were playing outside while my parents were doing yard work around our home in Mississippi, where we were living at the time. It was near the end of the day, the sun was setting with its golden rays, and I was swinging high on our swing set. I can't tell you what exactly happened, but all of a sudden I fell off the swing, my back hitting the ground flat and hard. I couldn't breathe. The fall had knocked the air out of my lungs and wasn't returning. I remember my dad coming to me quickly and assuring me I would be ok. It felt like minutes, but I know now it was only seconds before air entered my lungs fully again. I will never forget that moment of literally having the air knocked out of me. Little did I know that that feeling would come back when I was older, but it wouldn't be while doing something I enjoyed.

The physical reaction to hearing news that will change our lives forever is powerful. It's like falling off the swing set all over again. It's the panic, whether immediately or delayed, that tends to show up in full glory at some point. It's the moment your mind and body join together in full realization that something has happened. The moment when it's hard to breathe because you are in a state of shock.

I replay that phone call in the middle of the night when my brother let me know about my mom. This flashback comes up at times without warning, and I feel it again. I can't breathe. I panic. Racing thoughts. I can't comprehend my reality because how could she no longer exist in it. No. This can't be. I'm back on the floor on my hands and knees. "She's gone! She's gone!" Head to the ground. How small can I get in this moment? My husband is in disbelief. My oldest sees me. "Who's gone?" Tears are endless. It's a dream…no, a nightmare.

Then my logical brain sets in and reminds me I know this. I know that she is gone. I've done this before. I take a deep breath. Everything is ok. Sometimes it's like a loop occurs, and I feel it again. Like my body can't quite let go. Other times, I can calm my mind and body and go about my day being mindful of the residual feelings a flashback can bring.

I don't experience these memories as often as I used to. I find they only come around during special days, when I am back in the guest bed of my in-law's that I was sleeping in that night, or when I share details of my mom's death with others (or write a book about it!). These flashbacks are a part of the grief process I dread the most. They physically hurt because our fight or flight mechanism activates, and we know there is no relief to losing someone or something you can't get back. You can redirect your thoughts but the memory will still remain. Nowadays, researchers have found that trauma like this stays with us on a cellular level. This amazes me! Our bodies and minds are changed forever due to the events we experience.

The weight of a cargo ship sits on your chest while your heart races. Your brain shifts from reality to being back in time in the blink of an eye. A smell, a taste, a color, a sound, a feeling sets you back without you even being aware in the moment of the trigger. The tight chest that comes on purely due to a memory and not because a real threat is around you. The panic is powerful and humbling, but it is the natural progression of our brains accepting reality. If you find yourself panicking often or having full blown panic attacks, then it is time to talk to a doctor or psychiatrist about what help you can use in the meantime while you process what has happened. Sometimes our brains get stuck in the mental loop that causes us to physically react and assistance is needed.

If you find that what you are experiencing isn't at the level of needing professional support, use tools like:

- ✧ Taking deep breaths in to the count of four and out to the count of six
- ✧ Finding something (i.e. pillow, stuffed animal) or someone to hug to feel a sense of security
- ✧ List four things you see around you, four things you hear, and four things you physically feel to anchor yourself back into reality and calm your mind and body

THE PAIN

Think about a time you got bad news out of the blue. Where did you physically experience your response? More than likely you are going to say in your chest: your heart and your lungs. You may have started crying immediately or felt the tension in your head as you fought off your body's desire to cry. We experience a physical pain or discomfort when we receive information that is difficult for us to process. Interestingly, research has found that our brains process emotional pain and physical pain the same way.

I wanted to better understand what this physical response actually was, and when I discovered a condition called Takotsubo cardiomyopathy it all made sense. Takotsubo cardiomyopathy causes chest pain, shortness of breath, and dizziness in response to a major emotional or physical incident, all of which creates stress on the heart. It is a short-term phenomenon but actually changes the size of the heart's main pumping chamber. Literally, your heart physically responds to what you are hearing.

We drove into the driveway of my mom's home after an eight-hour flight and almost three hours of driving. I cried most of the trip, wrote a speech for mom's funeral, talked to my husband, and stared out the window. The physical shock had not hit again since the initial phone call from my brother, but I was in a state of mental shock. We pulled up, and I stayed in the car, dropped my head to the dashboard, and sobbed. Everything in me felt broken. It's like time stopped, or maybe I just wish it had.

It was hard to breathe as I cried there in the car. I didn't want to face it all. I finally looked up and all of my family was standing outside, waiting. They gave me permission to move at my own speed in this grief. Slowly, I stepped out of the car and hugged each one. As I walked into my mom's home, I felt cold and began to shake. My arms began tingling, and I felt dizzy. I tried not to panic over the physical response and kept saying "I'm just in shock" to myself to calm down. I was experiencing Takotsubo cardiomyopathy.

I had a minor version of the above symptoms when my parents shared they were separating. My world was completely going to change, and my mind and body didn't know how to process it all. My body reacted the way it could based on the stress of the moment. This physical response can occur when whatever you hear hits you like a ton of bricks and comes out of nowhere.

When I ask people about what some of the hardest parts of grief are, the physical response comes up often. Rightfully so. It is so hard, and it hurts...literally. Remember, though, this is your body responding appropriately to the information it is receiving. If you are scared, call your doctor or go to the emergency room. It's not in your head. There is a physical response taking place that can feel overwhelming and cause panic, and now that you know the name for it you are more in control.

Here are some tools you can use when you experience this pain:

- Drink a calming tea like chamomile or hawthorn
- Take a warm bath with Epsom salt
- Do some light stretching or relaxing yoga to help your muscles let go

THE LONGING

After Hurricane Katrina came through and destroyed my family's community in Mississippi, we all wondered how to adapt to this new normal. The landscape was completely different, and places I had been visiting since I was a baby were gone. I remember visiting my grandmother's home two years later and experiencing the longing for nature to go back to how it was. I missed the gorgeous oak trees and Spanish moss on Highway 90 along the beach. I craved the beautiful beaches without the new casinos on them that now had legal right to build there and the mini-golf spot I went to on dates. I wanted everything to look normal again. My heart longed for the comfort of what had always been and was no more.

Longing happens naturally in grief. We miss and long for the person, the place, our old normal, the dreams we had, or whatever has caused our grief. We physically feel the tug at our hearts. It's like a rope has wrapped itself around our heart pulling us while our body can't move. When we long, we can get stuck in the past.

Know that longing for the way things were is completely normal. It's when we stay in a mindset of missing what was and not being able to move forward that we create a more challenging grief process for ourselves. It's important that we guide ourselves back to our current reality. I like to do this by thanking those memories for still being there to help me to be grateful for what I do have. Then focus on what may come from this change. You are allowed to grieve and be grateful at the same time.

Though longing is another game of the mind, we can feel it in our bodies as well. As I said before, we can feel the tugging at our heart and the physical response to our sadness and anger of what we have to let go of. I recommend using guided meditations and a realistic gratitude practice to help with all of the physical responses to grief listed here. Again, if your physical response is so great that it scares you or is hard to manage at a certain point, please seek medical advice.

For a list of meditations to use, check out the resources at the end of this book.

Key Takeaways

- ✧ Panic occurs when the brain and body connect the information received and we struggle to believe or accept it.
- ✧ There is a very real physical response that occurs after an emotionally or mentally difficult experience and it has a name: Takotsubo cardiomyopathy.
- ✧ Longing is normal, but if we stay stuck in wishing things were the way they used to be, we won't see the beauty of our new reality.
- ✧ We can use tools such as meditation and gratitude to soothe these responses so that our body returns to its normal state.

CHAPTER 11

LONELINESS AND ISOLATION: WHEN WE BECOME HERMITS

Many of us associate grief with loneliness and isolation. It's true that this is a part of the grief path that we must all walk, but I was once challenged to think of isolation differently. Often, isolation is actually solitude. Solitude has a softer sound to it and is something we can benefit from. We all need the quiet, the pause from the rush of life, and to feel like we are on an island by ourselves. This space by ourselves is when we are able to powerfully reflect on our lives and what has happened to us. The reality is, though, that we are never actually alone.

We are going through
a very personal experience
that no one else will go through
in the same manner,
which makes us feel alone.

When we have such an individual experience, we feel separate, even if we were not alone in the situation. It makes us question all the bigger beliefs we have had in life, leaving our compass spinning. We can even get to the point of isolating ourselves so much that we start to see it as people not wanting to be around us and not the other way around. I have had countless clients share this feeling of being all alone, but then in the next breath tell me all the people they have checking in on them or calling them. Some of that is because we are not always ready to share our journey with others. That doesn't mean we are actually alone, though.

After my first miscarriage, the number of women who showed up in my life just to sit with me was amazing. Women that I didn't even realize had experienced miscarriages were sharing their stories. They all knew that I had to go through this journey individually, but they could be the outside support I could call when I needed it. As they shared their own stories with me, it gave me hope that this island I was standing on "all alone" would be worth exploring. Their miscarriages taught them about their own strength and helped them question the beliefs society and our families put on us related to failure and what a woman should and shouldn't do. I realized this grief process would help me grow a lot if I was willing to let it.

So much of grief is a private process, but we have to be careful that we don't end up isolating ourselves even further. What I mean is, occasionally row yourself from your personal island back to the mainland to connect with those around you. Tell them about your journey of grief. Be honest about your needs:

"Keep sending me texts even if I don't respond. They help."

"Please stop sending me quotes about grief. They sometimes make me feel worse. You can send me messages like 'How can I help today?' or send me videos of funny animals."

"Thank you for just listening and not trying to fix something that is not fixable."

We need the solitude in grief but we also need the connection of others who have walked this path before us. We must seek out that support and discern who is safe. Not everyone who has lost a parent is a safe person for me to talk to, but I don't know who is and who isn't until I start to talk and listen to them. Had I not shared with my community about losing my mom, people I only knew as acquaintances at the time wouldn't have come to be important parts of my life and my journey. It can be scary to involve others in your process, but it can have huge benefits as well. Set up a clear boundary of what you need and remind them it might change day to day. If they have walked a similar road to yours before, they will probably remember what it feels like and be willing to adjust.

Another reason we isolate ourselves is because we think "they won't understand." Again, this has some truth to it because it is your subjective experience, but to purposely isolate ourselves in our grief can actually negatively impact some of the stages of grief where we do need support. In the stage of sadness and depression, we can get trapped in the perpetual cycle it can cause when we fully remove ourselves from outside support. By having people around us to lift us up, we are able to shift out of this phase with more empowerment instead of feeling we "have to" move on because life is still going on whether we like it or not.

WHEN IT'S A FAMILY AFFAIR

Last year, I was interviewed on a podcast in which the interviewer shared how her family members were all experiencing grief differently around the death of her husband. Each had their own realities and memories that they held to be true, and it caused lots of issues. When we experience a loss or change in our family, it can cause major problems and divisions for some and bring others even closer together. What predicts which outcome will occur? Sometimes it's personality, sometimes it's healthy trust and communication dynamics already established in the family, and other times it's purely how each person handles grief, challenges, and negative emotions. In short, it can't fully be predicted, but you can definitely improve how you experience your grief and how you respond to others.

That being said, it is a lonely feeling when you experience a loss or change with others and can't grieve with them because how they are grieving either doesn't jive or is unhealthy. Due to the nature of grief, at some point, even a healthy grieving family will have members in it that feel alone in their grief. The key is communication in those situations.

Another issue that can come about is if the loss or change involves money. This can cause issues in families and isolation. Again, the key is communication, and I highly recommend having a mediator and therapist for support with issues around money.

Respect is a key part of grief when it impacts a family. Each of you will experience grief differently. This is completely normal. Some of you will make healthy choices to cope with your grief and express it. Others will not. More than likely you will all oscillate between the two. As infuriating as it can be when you are grieving differently from your loved ones, all parties need to respect each other even if you don't understand fully. Here's what I mean: Let's say your sister is in denial, your mother is angry, and you are in acceptance. Those three very different stages can naturally be combative. You try to get your sister out of denial calmly and lovingly. Your mom is verbally aggressive about it and attacking. You try to calm your mom down by helping her to better accept the situation. She lashes out at you for not letting her be angry and on top of that she is angry that you are not angry. See how this could become really damaging to relationships?

When we can respect how those around us are grieving, we don't try to push them into our corner of grief. We don't isolate them for being different, and we understand that our loneliness is only because we are grieving from a different place than our family members. It is not easy at all, and you may find there are times where you just have to put up a big boundary between you. This can be very helpful and healthy, even if your family members don't understand. Also know that they have the right to put up a boundary to you and how you are grieving. We tend to take it personally when someone creates a stronger boundary with us, yet we don't understand why, when the roles are reversed, others get so upset. I always say, try putting yourself in their shoes and think about what they must be feeling from their point of view. This helps with respect as well, even if it is still tough to fully understand.

WHEN SOMEONE'S NOT YOUR PERSON

I find many isolate themselves because they have been attacked for how they

feel, which causes them to experience rejection and shame. Here's a tip I learned long ago: We tend to speak to others from the framework of our own realities. So, if someone rejects how you are grieving, that says more about their issues than saying something about you. It's like when we are so worried about how we look because we wonder how others will judge us. Well, my friend, there is a high probability that no one is actually looking at you. They are self-consciously, constantly re-evaluating themselves out of fear of others looking at them. How many mean-girl movies need to come out for us to get this point?

When someone rejects how you grieve or what you need in your grief process, then they may not be the person to support you during this time. Even others who have experienced loss may not have been healthy grievers and can't understand what is going on as you choose to take healthy steps in your grief. We are a world that loves to share our opinions. Remember, though, that they are opinions and not facts.

Shame and guilt will try to get you to walk away from being healthy. It's the easier choice after all and keeps you from living life to the fullest. Try saying out loud when you find yourself getting trapped by shame and guilt either caused by your internal messages or messages others are telling you: "Sorry shame and guilt, but you no longer have power and control in my life. I choose to take healthy steps in grieving the way I need to."

Solitude is uncomfortable because many of us, even introverts who cherish solitude, are not comfortable being on our own completely. Again, there is nothing dangerous about having some time for solitude. Balance it with some visits to the mainland of social interaction, and you will move in this phase with more clarity.

Key Takeaways

- ✧ It is normal to feel all alone in your grief because it is a very subjective experience. Even family members in a family can experience the same loss differently.
- ✧ Be mindful not to sink into loneliness and isolation. Make sure to connect with someone who helps you feel supported in your grief whether they have experienced your situation or not.
- ✧ Not everyone is your person in your grief journey, but that doesn't mean you have to feel alone. Be willing to test people out for how they can support you in your grief process a little bit at a time to know if they are safe. Don't be hurt if they can't support you in the way you need. That's about them and not about you.

CHAPTER 12

HUMOR AS A TOOL: LAUGHING AT A FUNERAL

I can't remember a funeral with my family where we didn't laugh at some point. Maybe it's just how we cope, or it's a Mississippi thing, but I wouldn't have it any other way. Laughter is the best medicine for any negative emotion, in my opinion. It alleviates anger, rests the mind from worry and fear, and gets our head on straight by making us take a deep breath.

In fact, one of the reasons humor is such a great tool is that when you laugh, it makes you breathe so deeply. Have you ever had a deep belly laugh where you have to stop mid-laugh to take a breath before returning to laughing again? That's the best kind of laughter, and it's a great way to get as much oxygen in your lungs as possible in a short time. Believe me, your brain and body will thank you!

Why is humor an important tool in the grief process? Because it keeps us from going too deep into any phase of grief. It helps us feel some form of control and lightens the process.

It shifts the energy from staying stuck. One of the energy tools I teach in my grief healing sessions is how to be playful like a kid again with a simple technique. I have them put their hands up in front of them and imagine a ball between their hands while their eyes are closed. They can picture the ball any color, size, and consistency they want it to be. Then I have them play. They get to move it around how they want, tossing it up in the air, squishing it, moving it around between their hands. It allows their imagination to play in ways we as adults tend not to anymore. As the clients get to play, you can see them smiling and laughing. It feels silly at first, but then you really feel the ball is actually between your hands. We do this technique after addressing the deeper emotions attached to grief that are stuck in their bodies. I want to focus them back in the here and now after diving in deep, and the energy ball gets them focused on creating a feeling right in front of them.

As we go through a huge change right now in the world, humor is keeping so many of us going. Reading memes has become a new online coping skill. I believe we crave the lighter side of life when it gets too tough. But when is humor too much of an escape? When does it get in the way of working in our grief process? The answer is subjective. If you know you are not allowing yourself to have other emotions and are always responding with humor or watching/reading something funny, then this coping skill may have shifted into a defense mechanism like denial or escape addiction.

Another issue is that not everyone finds humor appropriate when grieving. They find it disrespectful, juvenile, and disconnected from what happened. This is more about their belief systems around what grief is and the rules of grief, instead of a personal attack on you if you find humor a helpful tool when grieving. You may be reading this thinking, "I find humor and laughter while grieving extremely inappropriate!" I would challenge you to take a deeper look and see what the reason for this is. Were you told that you were inappropriate if you laughed during serious matters as a kid? Did others who used humor during grief get "in trouble" with your family members? Where does this belief system come from?

CREATING VERSUS RECEIVING

It's not that it is wrong to believe that humor is inappropriate when grieving, but it's worth knowing why you may believe this. As I shared before, it is my professional and personal opinion that humor is an excellent tool for coping with grief. However, it shouldn't be forced on a person if they are not comfortable with it. It should also be pointed out that humor can come two ways: we create it ourselves, or we receive it.

When we create it ourselves, it is usually a comment or banter back and forth with someone to release the tension and discomfort, or to try and improve a challenging situation with a lighter mindset. Usually the humor is based around the event that happened. When we receive it, it can come in the form of watching a funny movie or video clip, reading a funny meme, or looking at funny photos. We don't have to create the humor ourselves but can still access it at any time. Many times in my grief I have leaned on this way of receiving humor to cope with and lighten my mood. I have recommended to many clients watching something funny before bed to help them relax and sleep better.

RELEASING THE PRESSURE COOKER

When I researched what causes some of us to use humor as a coping strategy and others not, I noticed a trend. Many share that they use humor to release the tension they feel from the emotions of grief. It's like they are a pressure cooker and just need someone to knock the top off to let out the steam. It's true that we can feel an internal pressure from an experience. Add a group of people around us feeling it too and you've amped up the pressure even more.

This is why so many use humor to relax. It can take our minds off the negatives in front of us. When we laugh together, we feel less alone. It's like we are given permission to feel a positive emotion during a challenging time and removes the feeling of isolation.

Here are some other reasons people use humor:

"It's so hard to process the unfathomable pain life can bring without recognizing the absurdity of it all! Some days you just have to laugh. During my first pregnancy we found out at a twenty-five week ultrasound that our little one had a fatal genetic anomaly. Such a rare condition it was like winning the lottery—but in reverse. After the initial shock wore off, we had to find the humor in that situation. It was just so crazy and weird we had to laugh sometimes. We cracked a lot of dark jokes prior to his birth and used a lot of humor in the funeral. It helped us blow off steam even though, yes, there were days crying in the fetal position on the bathroom floor. Grief was a full time job and non-linear at the same time." Lindsey, USA

"I don't really know why I do it. I've always cracked jokes when I'm nervous or uncomfortable. I'm particularly hilarious in medical situations or while giving birth. When writing my dad's eulogy,

there were parts that were really funny. It felt like the right way to honor him because he laughed a lot in his life. I'm certain that I've used humor since then to deflect from my own pain. If I'm laughing, I'm not crying, and if I'm laughing, you'll think I'm ok." Carrie, USA

"It's a very Australian thing to use humor to respond to difficult emotions. I definitely love a good cry and am not afraid to show emotion, but I also use humor to manage my own grief and to help others with theirs. I find that sharing funny stories about someone who has passed away can be a light way of letting people know you have not forgotten their loved one and an invitation to talk about that person or situation with someone who is clearly comfortable with it. It can be an opening for deeper sharing about a point of grief." Gabriel, Australia

Whether you are a lover of humor in grief or not, it cannot be denied that it has a place for many of us in our grief process. Remember: you get to make up your own grief rules anyways!

Key Takeaways

- ✧ Humor is a great coping skill for many to relieve the tension grief can create and to lighten the mood.
- ✧ If humor is not comfortable for you when going through grief, explore why not and what messages may have been sent to you in childhood about humor and challenging times.
- ✧ We can use humor as a coping skill in two ways: creating and receiving. Both are helpful in their own way when grieving.

CHAPTER 13

THE HOLIDAYS AND ANNIVERSARIES

I wrote about my grief often the first year after my mom's death. The holidays weren't as tough in the ways I had predicted they would be but were in ways I wasn't ready for. Such is life, right?

I thought that during holiday and family events I would struggle; however, I struggled the most in the quiet moments after. When I could finally think, my grief would show up and let me know it was still around. I would do a puzzle and remember when Mom and I would stay up late doing puzzles at my grandma's. I would help my oldest daughter with something and tell her "Grandma would have loved to be doing this with you right now."

There are some key things I learned about grief during the holidays that I have found to be true for many of my clients. First, your grief is present even if you don't feel it in the moment. You can be as busy as you want during the holiday season, but it only takes one song, one comment, or one trigger of a memory to bring your grief back to the forefront in your mind. Second, you must take time for yourself even when you feel like everything is ok. This is because parts of grief need to be nurtured along the way of they rear their ugly heads in not so fun ways. Since grief is always present, all you need to do during these special times is take 10-15 minutes to journal or check in with yourself and see how you are feeling. What does your grief need you to know right now? Like literally ask it: "Grief, what do you need me to know right now?" This helps you get more present with what your mind and body will be telling you it needs. Maybe it's just having some quiet time every day for a walk or connecting with a safe person to share how you are. It can be very simple, but when we don't take the time, we can get extremely reactive. One Christmas, I remember my husband making a comment about something I forgot, and I exploded. How dare he not see what I was going through and everything I was trying to do. The poor guy didn't stand a chance against my grief. It was then I realized I didn't make time for myself to make sure I was ok.

Third, I can't emphasize enough how important it is that you have people in your life who understand you. You may be in a room with a ton of people during the holidays and not feel like you can be your true self, so make sure you have that person you can call or text to express what you are feeling. You may even find an online support group to be the most helpful instead of one person. I have talked to several people who have lost a pet, and they found online groups the most supportive and encouraging as they grieved their loss. Lastly, the actual day of a holiday can be a great distraction. It's the calm afterward that can put you face to face with your sadness and, sometimes, in an even greater amount than expected. I always compare this experience to riding a roller coaster. You have all this excitement and a rush going on and then you get off and about five minutes later you feel this drop. You may get a little moody, tired, and struggle to make decisions. You are coming off the high of the holiday time and the drop naturally happens to us all, but add in grief and the drop feels like a bad carnival ride.

The first holidays and anniversaries after a loss can be the hardest. (Remember, there is no rule to this, so it may be different for you.) This does not mean that subsequent years will be easy, but they more than likely will get more manageable as you navigate how you respond in your grief. You may even find at times you forget, and you may even feel guilty for doing so. Remember that anniversaries are special, but they don't have to be focused on just that day.

THE POWER OF TRADITIONS AND RITUALS

I found there was one key way to help me and my clients during holidays and anniversaries: creating new traditions and rituals. One mom I talked to always planted seeds for flowers on the anniversary of her mom's death. I take my daughters to get ice cream on my mom's birthday every year. Another friend plans something special with a close friend on her old wedding anniversary even years after her divorce. New traditions help us acknowledge the difference and show respect for the magnitude of change it created in our lives.

Sometimes there is a catalyst to our grief in which creating a new tradition doesn't make sense but creating a ritual does. When a dream doesn't come to fruition, a ritual might be a better thing to do. For example, let's say you are a parent of a young adult who comes out as gay. Some of the grief work you may go through is letting go of what you pictured for their future. You may have imagined their wedding and how it would be when you had grandkids. Initially, this may seem like something you have to completely let go of, but over time, you will find that the dream has become even more beautiful because it has shifted to fit your child's wishes versus just yours. This is where a ritual would help. Let's say you start down the path of negative thinking about what won't happen for you and your child. A ritual might be to write it down and put it in a box imagining you are removing it from your mind. At the end of the month you could burn all the fears and negative thoughts that came up for you. Or you might write down three positive things that will come from your child living their true identity each time a negative thought comes up.

Rituals are beautiful ways
to release and grow
toward acceptance.

I use burning rituals every year. On New Year's Eve, I write down all the things I want to let go of and release from the year. All the hurtful things I have held on to, the times I did things I am frustrated at myself for, and the things that happened as normal life occurrences that I didn't enjoy. I fill up as many pages as I want and then before midnight burn them. I use this ritual as well in my grief healing groups. The students, after working for a couple weeks on their grief, write down all the things about a particular situation they want to let go of. Then, when they are ready they burn the paper and imagine it being released from their minds and bodies. One student chose to tie her papers to a rock and throw them in a local river. Water was more impactful to her than fire, and the ritual became even more powerful because she personalized it.

Here are other traditions and rituals people have found helpful:

Donating to a cause

Lighting a sky lantern

Coming together with family or friends for a special meal

Planting a tree or plant

Creating a photo album of your best memories

Walking or running in a place significant to the change or loss

"I have a Pandora bracelet celebrating my journey as a mom with charms that represent different milestones for my girls. I have heart spacers mixed throughout to honor the babies we lost during IVF. It's just a quiet reminder for me." Melissa, USA

"Every year on my cousin's birthday our family does random acts of kindness. We've paid for the car behind us in the drive thru, left enough money for two families at a buffet, given to the Red Cross, etc., and always in his name." Brie, USA

IS IT NECESSARY TO REMEMBER?

I have always found my body responds with grief symptoms before my mind does when anniversaries are coming. I become more tired, more reactive, more emotional. Then I look at what the date is on the calendar and see that an anniversary is coming up. The days before and even some days after can be really challenging. I think it's the anticipation leading up to the days before and the realization the days after an anniversary that cause the difficulty.

Though grief is always a part of us, there are times where we feel it more. It's amplified by these special days, and the days before and after are like parentheses around a heightened grief period. I know, though, that there are some who keep busy and rush right through the day of an anniversary not even realizing it. It's like their brain knows to escape reality by keeping a long to-do list. They often notice after the fact (even days later) and feel an immense amount of guilt over this.

But is it necessary for everyone to feel heavy amounts of grief on an anniversary? Is it a requirement to stop and honor that day in particular? Obviously, many who skip over an anniversary feel guilt, so there seems to be an unspoken rule about it. However, I struggle to believe this must be. Can't we honor the loss, change, move, or experience whenever and however we want? That's the beauty of writing our own grief rules.

Let's also give ourselves permission to miss the anniversary without experiencing guilt afterward. You may have missed the date subconsciously on purpose, but it's no reason to beat yourself up over it. The key is to remember our minds like to protect us, and if we are concerned that something will upset or hurt us, we will avoid it like the plague. When you notice this has occurred for you, you can smile and thank yourself for protecting your feelings. Then, remind yourself how capable you are of feeling anything that comes up around an anniversary.

Key Takeaways

- ✧ Creating traditions and rituals around anniversaries and holidays helps us honor the loss, change, move, or experience.
- ✧ The days leading up to and after a holiday or anniversary can be challenging as well (sometimes more challenging than the actual day itself).
- ✧ It is not necessary to remember an anniversary because honoring an experience can happen any time you want.
- ✧ If you experience guilt around forgetting an anniversary, remember it is your mind protecting you and not something to beat yourself up over. Release the pressure and remind yourself that you are capable of feeling the difficult emotions that surround a special day.

CHAPTER 14
THE HELPERS

Journal entry, December 2019: *I am determined that 2020 will be a year that I do not hear "I'm so sorry."*

This is a hard chapter to write because it addresses the help that people believe they are giving us in our time of deep grief. I write this knowing that I have said these things before to others before I knew better, and you probably have as well. My hope with this chapter is to use our own grief experiences to take a deeper look at what we can say to someone who is currently experiencing grief.

First my mom died, then about nine months later we had our first miscarriage and then about six months after that we had our second miscarriage. What was the number one phrase I heard in 2019? "I'm so sorry."

"I'm so sorry for your loss."

"I'm so sorry this keeps happening to you."

"I'm so sorry you are going through this."

I appreciated the sentiment, but as you can imagine, I heard this phrase more than I would have liked. I began the new year believing I could stop people from needing to say this phrase to me. Did I mention I have some control issues? I didn't want people to need to have sympathy for me anymore. It started to feel like I was being stuffed into the grief box over and over and over again. I wanted out!

This chapter is going to address what not to say and what to say when someone is grieving. It may seem a little out of place in this book since I am talking about your grief healing journey, but I realized in my own healing process the importance of learning how to communicate with others when they are grieving too. Doing this also helped me take it less personally when someone really upset me while I was grieving. I like to think they just didn't know any better...we'll go with that theory for now.

GOING BEYOND "I'M SORRY"

As I write this, we are in 2020 and the world is in quarantine, facing a global pandemic. Many are going through grief: losing family members, grieving the loss of normal life and not knowing how long this will take, losing jobs, and grieving the end of their school year that involved canceled rites of passage like school dances and graduations. I find myself almost writing to someone each week with "I'm so sorry," but I stop myself. I remind myself that this isn't just the year I don't want to hear "I'm so sorry" but also the year I want to say more than this phrase. I want to let them know they are not alone. I want them to know they have support if they need it. And I want them to know that these are normal feelings to experience.

I started saying and writing things like, "My heart is with you during this time. I am here when you need me and will be thinking of you. What you are feeling is completely normal." Reflecting on what I needed, I remembered that people taking the time to honor what I was feeling or thinking was so helpful. People normalizing my experience had a big impact as well. It didn't help to hear people say, "I can't imagine what it would be like to go through this," though I realized they were trying to reflect that they were not sure what to say.

The most hurtful responses were things like, "You must be devastated," "How horrible this time is for you," and "You poor thing." It was like I was being told how I should be feeling, how I should view what was happening to me, and that I was a victim to life's circumstances. Whoa! Talk about the rules of grief hitting you repeatedly in the head till you follow them. We often try to imagine what it is like for the other person and think we are being supportive. In reality we are pushing our belief systems about grief and experiences on them.

What if we said things like:

"How are you feeling?"

"How has this experience been for you?"

"What help can I offer you during this time?"

"What is helping right now and what isn't?"

Did you notice the trend? These are questions to show support versus statements of what we think we should say. They give the griever the opportunity to be free in their response, even if they don't take it. Most of us are not used to having someone be so open to listening to us. People struggle to impose their negative feelings or dark thoughts on others, so if the person you want to support doesn't share a lot you can encourage them by saying you are willing to listen no matter what they have to say.

There were some people I was ready to open up to and others I wasn't, but knowing that I had the freedom to and that the person wasn't going to put me in their "this is how grief should look" box made it easier to talk to them later on. Remember this: if they don't share with you right away, you are just planting the seeds for them to feel safe so they can in the future.

PUT YOUR WORDS INTO ACTION

Now, I must add, if you don't want to sit with someone else in their grief that is ok too. Stick with the first two questions in the above examples and stay there. Don't offer what you can't give. I always laughed inside when people would offer to bring meals but then there were so many stipulations about when and what. I felt like I was doing more of the work for something they had offered me. Be honest with yourself and check in that your good intentions are more than just intentions but a real desire to follow through with the help.

When we offer help to someone, we must be willing to put our words into action. It is one hundred percent ok to have to change your availability after offering it, but make sure it is clear that you need to do this. "I know I said I could bring you a meal this week, but things became more chaotic than I expected. May I order something to be delivered to your home or should we reschedule for next week?" Sticking with our offer of help but changing up the way it happens is completely understandable.

If you are the one grieving and someone starts to fall through on their offer, do your best not to personalize it. I have noticed that often when it didn't work out for someone to help or be there for me, there was a bigger reason for it. Trust that the help you need will come from the right person. Also, don't be afraid to reach out when you need help and think about who you would really like to be there to support you. Sometimes we reach out to those who are fast to respond but are not the best support for us personally. Remember: not everyone is your person. Make sure you really reflect on what you need and who could really be there for you the best way possible.

If we are close with the person who is going through grief, sometimes we know them better than they know themselves. We know our friend or family member is the type to say they are fine when they really are not. I once had a friend check in on me, and I gave the same old response of "I'm good." She still came by my house with a special treat and dropped it off. The friend didn't stay but knew I needed to feel loved in that moment. We often throw out the window all the things we know about a person when they go through a challenging time. Maybe they are the type to separate themselves when something bad happens and you know they just need a reminder once or twice a week by text message that you are there. Or maybe they need someone to come do their laundry so they can take a nap and you just have to show up and tell them what's what. Trust the history you have with the person to be a good guide on how to support them during their grief.

WHAT NOT TO SAY

THE TOUGH-IT-UP RESPONSES:

"Get over it."

"You should be over this by now. It's been almost a month."

Any sentence that starts with *"At least..."*

"He/She is/was already old... it was expected..."

"Honey, it's not so bad. You don't have to cry."

"You're young. You can have another."

"It could have been worse."

The classic responses when someone is more a thinker than a feeler.

What do I mean by this? Well, some of us are feelers. We are in touch with our emotions. While others of us are thinkers and more logical. I am not saying one is better than another, but this is a time when the logical-minded person or thinker doesn't shine at their best. The tough-it-up response is trying to engage the inner warrior in the person so that they become "stronger" in the face of what they are dealing with. In reality, it discounts what the person is feeling and makes you an unsafe person for them to go to when they need support.

THE COMPARISON RESPONSES:

"My sadness was greater than yours is right now."

"Well, so and so got to hold their baby, so I'm sure that was a lot harder."

I am going to be honest. I am not sure what benefit anyone gets out of comparing their grief stories. Maybe someone thinks it helps give perspective to the other person, but it actually discounts what they are feeling as well. Only share your story if it will help the person, and definitely don't compare your response with theirs.

THE RELIGIOUS RESPONSES:

"They are in a better place."

"Everything happens for a reason."

"There will be more babies where that one came from."

"God just wanted another angel."

Growing up in a religious family, I am very familiar with these responses from the church community. There is no easy way to approach this so I will address it purely from a place of love. There are phases of grief where these comments are not helpful. They will drive the person to anger. It's hard to know what phase a person is in, so it's best to let them make comments like this themselves. If they make a comment like this, it gives you permission to support what they are saying.

LET'S MAKE YOU FEEL GUILT AND SHAME RESPONSES:

"Why did you shut us out? We wanted to be there for you."

"Do you think it was because you…?" (placing blame on the person for why the event happened)

"I'm surprised you are doing so poorly. You are a counselor. You should be coping better!"

Another group of responses in which I am unsure how the helper thought it was appropriate to respond the way they did. Again, these are real responses members of my community experienced while going through grief. The first response above might occur if you need to put up boundaries with others and they don't get it. Often, they don't understand because they have not gone through a challenging time where boundaries were needed. This doesn't mean you did anything wrong. This is their own issue and shouldn't be put on your shoulders. Please do your best to ignore it.

The second response is our innate desire to figure out the root cause of something. However, in this case, it is inappropriate. You are not there to figure this out or try to solve why something occurred. When we do this, we are trying to resolve our own curious minds and find solutions. By doing so, we add guilt and shame to the griever's experience.

The last response can occur when we assume someone should be able to handle a loss or change better based on their profession. We definitely do not need to say this to them, even if we are thinking it. It does not help them feel stronger, rather it creates a feeling that they are less than they should be. Shaming someone is not supporting them in their grief.

Lastly, there are two more things not to say or do when you hear someone is grieving:

1. Don't tell them about how others have it worse than them and that they should be grateful for what they do have.
2. Don't dump your grief on them if you are grieving too, especially if it is over the same situation.

These are about boundaries. The first one typically occurs because we want them to not feel alone, but in reality, it's like overloading them with more information. When my mom died, several people told me about so-and-so who also had died recently. It was awful. It felt like all these people were dying because that's what so many were talking to me about. Now, if you went through something similar, you can share this but don't go into detail unless they ask. Also, definitely don't use the phrase "I know how you feel" no matter what experience you have had. No one can actually know how another is feeling fully. Again, we don't want the person to feel alone so we say these things. More times than not, the person is not comforted to hear this.

The second issue with having no boundaries is when we dump our own grief on someone who is grieving. I wonder if this occurs because it feels like the person we are sharing with is in the same boat. The problem is exactly that. They are going through a difficult time as well, so leaning on them for support or venting to them when they probably already feel depleted is a sure fire way to hurt that relationship. Find someone else to be your support.

WHAT TO SAY

So, what should people say? This is a tough question to answer. I have already shared in this chapter some ideas, but let's go further. Often, if we stop and think about the person we are responding to we may be able to pick up on some key ways to respond. You can start with questions: *How are you? How can I be a support for you right now?* Then you can listen to what they have said and respond from that. Or if they seem to be giving you short answers, take that as a sign they are not open to talking to you further. Let them know you will support them however they need it, even if it's from a distance. Give them permission to take as long as they need and remind them they don't have to respond to you if they don't want to.

Here are some more suggestions from those in my online community who have gone through grief on what to do and/ or say:

"Continue checking up on me after *the funeral. So often, people who are grieving are inundated with phone calls, social media messages, text messages, visitors, tons of food, etc. in the time leading up to the funeral. However, everyone goes back to their normal lives after the funeral and I'm left here all alone dealing with grief."*

"Just be with me. Not feeling the need to fix it or say the right thing. Just be there and check in months after. Because that's when it really gets hard."

"Say 'I don't have answers but I'm here to listen, or just be with you in silence if that helps' and also 'Would you like me to help you [insert chore here]?'"

"To just include *me."*

"Say 'I'm stopping by with a coffee and a hug for you.'"

"Say 'How's your heart today?'"

"Say 'I'd love to hear one of your favorite memories of (person), if you're up for sharing.'"

"Say 'Dinner is being delivered tonight/tomorrow. What time would you like it to arrive?'"

"Say 'Here's some homemade lasagna.' In all seriousness. Words are never adequate to a heavy loss. Food is better."

These lessons and tips are great for adults to learn. It's the responsibility of parents and caregivers to raise the next generation to be kind, respectful, and appropriately feel and respond to grief. First, we do the work to improve ourselves, by doing the next generation observes. This is the best way to create change when it comes to grief and how we respond. Second, we make sure to teach children an emotional vocabulary that allows them to express with words what they are feeling. Third, we respect that words will not always be able to be found so we also teach them healthy coping strategies like creating art, playing music, building something, letting out aggression in safe ways, and using exercise or sports in positive ways to release physical tension from grief.

When it comes down to grief, we will all say or do something wrong. Though it's normal, it's not a reason to give up growing and improving how you respond. We should not beat ourselves up if we have said some of the above comments. Use the information above to inform yourself for the future. Heck, share it with someone in your life who needs to read it as well. I bet you read this and thought, "______ needs to read this!" Just a side note on this: it's great you want to teach someone else how to respond more appropriately to grief, but recognize that they may not be emotionally ready to understand what it means to actually support someone in their grief. I always say, we have our physical age, our mental age, and our emotional age, and they can all be different! Hence why we can't always expect someone older than us to "get it" if they are emotionally stuck due to their own past.

Key Takeaways

- ✧ You more than likely have been or will get hurt or frustrated by a response someone has to your grief. Please don't let this overtake your focus on your own grief healing. Their responses are about their grief rules, and they don't need to affect yours.

- We all want to be helpers, but it can be challenging at times to follow through with the support. Make sure you don't offer unless you really mean it.
- Remember that if someone doesn't follow through with the support they offer you, it's probably for the best and not a reflection on you.
- Positive ways to respond involve asking how someone is, being present with them, checking on them weeks and even months later, and offering to help them with tasks that may be adding stress to their lives.

CHAPTER 15

GRIEF ISN'T PRETTY, SO LET'S STOP APOLOGIZING

I've addressed this topic before, but it truly deserves its own chapter. So here it is. For thirteen years I have worked with people as a counselor and transformative grief guide. For thirteen years people have apologized to me for crying in session. It baffles me. Something we all do in our lives, and yet we feel the need to apologize for it when it's done in the presence of someone else...even a therapist. Why?

I sought to understand this societal norm, and it's about us more than the other person. We:

- ✧ are embarrassed.
- ✧ are ashamed.
- ✧ believe we are showing weakness.
- ✧ believe we are imposing on the other.

I have never heard of a person saying, "Hey, can you stop because I am uncomfortable with you crying?" Yet we apologize and assume there is something wrong with crying in front of someone else. Now, don't get me wrong. There are probably times where you have felt uncomfortable when someone cried in front of you and you definitely have had times when you have made someone uncomfortable. However, it's ok for someone to be uncomfortable because you are crying. I believe when we go through these experiences with someone else, no matter if we are the one crying or the support person, it helps us grow and learn how to better handle these situations in the future.

I have started saying "Thank you" when I am crying and someone sits with me. I realized I don't want to feel ashamed or embarrassed anymore about crying no matter what my face looks like. Emotions are not weakness, and it's time to remove this belief from our systems and our society. We all feel them, and we all need to express them. So, let's get on board with growing more comfortable with emotions.

BOYS VERSUS GIRLS

Historically, there has been a belief that emotions and being "emotional" are a sign of being feminine, which clearly in history hasn't always been seen as a strength. (Sorry Joan of Arc, we know you tried!) Men are told they are crying like a "little baby" or like a "girl." We are taught from early on to toughen up, be strong, and ignore how we feel by doing something to take our minds off of it. From childhood, we are taught to not cry, especially not in front of people. As I write this, it breaks my heart for my girls and their generation. If we don't change this mentality about emotions they will have to continue the work we should have been doing.

For example, I find it interesting that when a little girl cries many respond by hugging her and telling her it will be ok or that things are not so bad. However, when a little boy cries, those same people say things like "ok, that's enough crying" or "you're just fine" and encourage the boy to stop crying much quicker than they would a girl. There has been a huge movement in the last ten years to teach parents how to help their sons be emotionally intelligent, and in doing so, allowing them to cry without a "that's enough" response. We must do more though.

When I interviewed men in my community about how they were raised to understand their emotions, there were a variety of answers. Some shared that emotions are a sign of weakness, especially sadness and grief. Others talked about not feeling like there was space for them to express themselves in their family, especially if they had a sister or very emotional mom. Then there were a few who were able to say that emotions were welcomed in their home, but they learned to hide how they felt in school. It's not just in our homes that we must work on creating this change; it's also in our kids' everyday life—at school, in sports and clubs, and in community events. The more boys are exposed to grown men who are able to express emotions in healthy ways the more they will be comfortable expressing their emotions as well. Again, this means we adults need to do the work so we are ready to model the change we want to see.

We want to teach our children to grieve in a healthy way, but we are still healing old wounds from not having had that same freedom of expression. Generations have been told to toughen up, leading to a lot of the problems with physical and mental health issues that we see today. When we finally start working on healing these issues through teaching the next generation a healthier way to express their emotions, we see real change in families and society as a whole.

GRIEF ISN'T PRETTY

Emotions are not always pretty. They don't always make us feel good or comfortable. However, just like grief, they are important. They teach us to be aware of ourselves and our surroundings. Look at fear: it's a tool for information. We are scared so we need to gather more information, remove ourselves from a situation, or stand up for ourselves. It is telling us something is not right. There is an imbalance. Thank goodness for fear!

Fear can also show us areas of healing that still need to occur. Getting into a new, healthier relationship can still create fear if your last one was abusive. It shows that you need to move slowly and do the grief work and healing to be able to feel safe again. It protects you so you know how to proceed. Not always to stop but to lead with caution and take time for healing and discernment.

Grief can cause us to be reactive from a place deep down inside of us that we didn't know had a voice. It can make the sweetest, never-hurt-a-fly person more honest and blunt. It can make the biggest socialite a hermit. I found that it made me not always pleasant to be around, but I needed to forgive myself for that more than those around me.

My mother's first birthday after her death was surreal. She would have been 58, and I felt lost on what to do. Recently, I reread this journal entry, and it's a good example of the roller-coaster ride we can go on in grief just in one day. Here's what I wrote:

> *Today. Hmmm…still not sure how to describe it, but I know that it is important that you see all sides of grief.*
>
> *Today, Mom would have been fifty-eight. We would have called her and sung to her. I would have sent a gift, maybe some flowers. She would have shared about the start of her day and what she planned to do for dinner. I probably would have texted her throughout the day, checking in to make sure she was doing special things for herself.*
>
> *I don't get to do that today.*
>
> *Today, I started with a smile, and as the day progressed, I felt numb. Then the anger hit again. The deep sadness that is masked by anger is no stranger. It's actually the most comfortable stage of grief for me.*
>
> *I was impatient with the girls, snappy at my husband, and felt completely overwhelmed. I didn't try to fight it or hide it. I knew I wouldn't cause any permanent damage by showing my emotions today. Plain and simple: I was hurting.*

Grief isn't pretty. It doesn't feel good. It makes you look at parts of yourself you don't like. It makes you face reality like a cold shower. Some days are filled with anger that end in tears when the day is done. Today is that day for me.

I miss you, Mama. Happy birthday. Love you.

I'll write it again so it's clear: grief isn't pretty. Period. It doesn't matter what bow you try to adorn it with. It isn't meant to be pretty. It's meant to be challenging and to help you grow deeper and wider into the person you were meant to be. It's here to help us truly live life to the fullest. Just like crying in public, it's not something we need to apologize for or be ashamed of. It's not a weakness to experience grief. It's a normal part of the human experience.

Our grief can come out in overreactions in difficult moments and intense emotions that others don't always understand. Know that not everyone will be able to sit with your emotions in these moments because they haven't sat with their own yet. This doesn't mean something is wrong with you. It just means you're hurting. We can't always predict when we will react in the thick of grief, and that's ok. We shouldn't be expected to always keep it together. That's just unrealistic to be honest. When we start the grief healing process, though, we notice that those big emotions and reactions start to become tamer, and we can sense them in advance. We know how to respond, and we are able to know who it's safe to show them to.

Grief has so many sides to it that "pretty" isn't a good adjective for it. I like to think of grief as beautiful—of course not in the classical sense of beauty. It's beautiful in its fullness, in how it shapes us. It's beautiful in its complexity. It's beautiful in what it can create in and around us.

Grief isn't pretty. It's beautiful.

Key Takeaways

- We don't have to apologize for our grief just like we don't have to apologize for crying in front of someone.
- Gender differences in how we are allowed to express negative emotions have created generations of people who struggle to grieve now.
- We can empower the next generation, no matter what their gender is, to express their grief in healthy ways giving them the freedom to experience what they are feeling.
- It is normal to be reactive and have intense emotions when deep in grief. Not everyone will be ready to receive this though.

Real Grief Stories

My mom was diagnosed with terminal cancer and passed away three months later. This altered the trajectory of my life.

What is the deeper meaning you have found in your grief?

I've come to accept death in a way that has allowed me to embrace life more fully. It triggered me to take more full advantage of the present and the life in front of me rather than put off my dreams for some future time.

What special or powerful experience led you to find this meaning?

I was able to go through the stages of grief while she was still present. I intuitively knew that she was passing away, despite the medical professionals not giving us any such prediction. Because I was able to get to acceptance while I still had time with her, it allowed me to have conversations I couldn't have had if I was in one of the earlier stages. Being with my mom during her last weeks here also helped awaken me to spirituality and a world that I was previously closed off to.

Amanda, 38, Costa Rica

CHAPTER 16
THE POWER OF AND

Very quickly in my grief process I realized that it was a myth that we can only feel one emotion at a time. It didn't make sense to me when I would think, "If I'm sad and grieving, I can't be happy or excited too." I felt stuck in this old belief. It didn't fit the experience I was having, and it wasn't realistic. I recognized that I was more worried about what others would think if I expressed or showed other emotions, especially positive ones. If I went out with friends and shared pictures of me being happy and laughing: Would people think I was over the death of my mom? Would they think I wasn't grieving her loss properly? Would they think I was trying to escape?

I realized this issue wasn't about me but about other people and their own restrictions of grief. It was not fair to me, and it's not fair to you to be stuck in the "you are allowed only one emotion at a time" prison. This goes back to those pesky rules of grief. It also can be a double standard as we look at someone else's life and judge how they are handling their grief and the choices they are making compared to how we choose to handle our grief and the choices we make. I know I have been guilty of this many times in my life. This also addresses the false belief that a grieving person can only really be grieving if they are expressing and acting like it 24/7. (But then again that might be *too* much!)

This rule didn't fit my experience, and it hasn't fit for most people I have met. For those who are stuck with this belief system, feelings of guilt and shame trap them. The shoulds keep them from growing and experiencing life. The worries about others' opinions keep them acting the way others expect, and they lose out on opportunities that grief provides when expression is natural.

WHAT DOES AND LOOK LIKE IN GRIEF?

I can smile AND be sad. I can cry AND be happy. I can have a fun time with friends AND have moments where I pause and feel empty because life isn't what I expected it to be. I can celebrate my daughters' birthdays with a smile on my face AND grieve that my mother isn't able to be there in person ever again. I can enjoy our three girls AND grieve that there are two babies that I lost.

> Thank goodness we are capable of complex emotions because grief is made more beautiful and more beneficial by feeling multiple ways at once.

It teaches us how amazing our minds and bodies are and gives us permission to shift and change whenever we want. My thirty-fifth birthday was a few weeks after my first miscarriage, and there was a part of me that wanted to stay in bed and do nothing. A bigger part of me, however, wanted to be with my friends, to laugh and joke around. I wanted to take a sip of conversations that were light-hearted and silly to cool the inner pain I felt. We did end up having a get together for my special day. One friend showed up with a hula hoop, another with a new running outfit, and another with an invitation for a girls' night out for some fun. Gifts that reminded me that I still get to live AND grieve the losses and changes in my life.

The power of AND allows you to experience all of the emotions and thoughts in the presence of real life. You can laugh at a funny video two minutes after crying all afternoon. You can feel so much love for someone AND be angry at them. You can enjoy the wedding of a friend AND feel the abandonment of your spouse leaving. You can love the new city you live in AND miss your old home deeply. You can feel fulfilled in your career AND miss spending more time with your kids. You get the right to feel both, and no one has the right to take that from you.

When you start to hear the voice of doubt, guilt, and shame that says you are only allowed to feel one emotion at a time and that you must worry about what others think of how you are grieving, please give yourself permission to laugh in that moment. Laugh at the weight that wants to pull you down but has nothing to do with your grief at all. You don't need extra weight on you in grief, so laugh it away. You've got some AND emotions to feel, and there is no room for doubt, guilt, and shame because of how others judge.

GRIEF AND GRATITUDE

My favorite AND combination: grief and gratitude. What a powerful combination that tends to be misunderstood by so many! Somehow, many people started believing that we need to experience only gratitude in order to push away grief. Well, sorry, that's not how grief works...I hope you get that by now. If we only focus on what we are grateful for, it's simply a bandage on the wound. Logically it makes sense: distract the mind with something positive, with what one has versus doesn't have. However because of the power of AND, that is not how this works. You will still come back to feelings of grief after and even possibly during moments of gratitude.

When we add another child into our family, it can create mixed emotions for the parents. We can start out excited that the new child is coming, and then we start to think about the child or children we already have. Can we love another child as much? What if this negatively impacts our current family dynamic? There is a panic that we might "screw up" our existing child by adding more. Once the new child comes, we see that our ability to love is infinite and beautifully unique for each child. We also see how adaptable and resilient children are to new things in life. Thank goodness for this!

If you have fertility issues, this brings up different feelings. I can't tell you how many women who have lost a baby or had fertility issues I have heard share stories about people telling them to be grateful rather than grieve. Things like, "Be grateful that you have kids already even though you lost one," "Be grateful you are so young so you can keep trying," or "Be grateful that at least one of the twins survived." I shake my head at these because they completely discount the loss and challenges a woman goes through. Sure they can be grateful for these things, but can't they grieve as well? Are they not allowed to be hurting, disappointed, anxious, angry, and sad?

Imagine you are at the edge of a cliff looking down, feeling beat up by life. Everything is overwhelming. Everything hurts. I come up to you and say, "Hey there! Look up at the sunrise. Don't you see the sunrise? Look how pretty it is. Stop looking down. There's a sunrise!" You might glance up at it and see it, but you are still sure as heck going to look back down at that cliff. You are at the edge of it after all! However, if I built a bridge from one side of the cliff to the other and said, "I know you feel overwhelmed and alone. I am here for you when you need it. This all just sucks! When you are ready, there's a sunrise I want to show you and a bridge for you to safely walk on so you can see it while also knowing the cliff is there." You would be able to experience your grief and gratitude together.

It's ok to see the sunrise and the cliff and fully experience both. I find that gratitude is a much fuller and deeper experience when I am grieving. It's like I am able to see both sides of life giving me a greater appreciation for it. When someone tries to make you only see the sunrise, and especially if they guilt trip you into it, feel free to remind them of the power of AND. You are able to be grateful for what you have AND also grieve what you don't. This will help you take back control of those moments to walk taller and stand stronger in your truth.

What if you want to feel gratitude while grieving but are struggling? If it's hard to find something happy in your new normal, start small. My gratitude practice now involves me writing down a few macro things like my health, my family, my friends and some micro things like dandelions, rainy days, cake, and my favorite color. What we can be grateful for comes in all shapes and sizes, so if gratitude for the big-picture things is tough right now, start with the little, much like a child would look at the world. "I am grateful for that breeze right now. I am grateful for that cloud that looks like a dinosaur. I am grateful for the plant on my desk that I get to look at during my work day." Don't judge yourself for what you write or say. Just allow yourself to be grateful.

A friend recently shared that after a big move to a new country, she has a practice of writing down the things she likes in the new country that didn't exist in the home she longed for. Let me set the scene better: she's American, lived in Germany for several years, and recently moved to Japan. Let's talk about culture shock to the max. So, instead of grieving her new reality, she writes down and makes mental notes of the things she likes. It can include a different salad dressing not available in German shops, the new terrain in the nearby neighborhood, and the fun trips the family can take to go on new adventures, like where ninjas train! Her boys are in heaven! She realized that there are positives in every new reality, but you have to get out of thinking the old way was better and start to be open to what is now.

EXAMPLE OF A REALISTIC GRATITUDE PRACTICE:

Today, I feel (list all of your emotions, including the negative ones or your "cliffs") AND (there's your bridge) I am grateful for (it can be something small or big and you get to decide how long the list is that day...this is your sunrise).

Let the power of AND free you to feel what you need to and want to. Release that nagging feeling that you need to worry what others think of you. Your grief is yours and no one can tell you how to feel or experience it. Thank goodness for the power of AND!

Key Takeaways

- We are allowed to experience multiple emotions at once while grieving.
- Often when we struggle with AND emotions it is because of our fear of how others will perceive us or old rules on how grief should look. It's time to shed the old rules!
- You can grieve and be grateful in the ways you want to be. No one should press upon you their own thoughts/belief systems of how thinking positively with gratitude can wash away feelings of grief. It doesn't work that way.
- Gratitude can be for small and basic things or big and expansive ideas. You get to decide.

Real Grief Stories

I was a young single mother to a precious little boy who was swept off her feet by a caring, loving man. We started our blended family, and it was literally a dream come true for myself and my son. However, it was torn apart when my partner attempted suicide, which lead to our divorce and the ending of our family we had worked so hard to create.

What is the deeper meaning you have found in your grief?

It taught me that the hardest moments in your life, can be the greatest moments of your life. It will humble you; it will make you appreciate so many things you took for granted it; and it will ultimately make you a better person.

What special or powerful experience led you to find this meaning?

It was the moment, holding my son, that I realized I wasn't broken. I was whole. I was enough. It was the fact that despite everything I never stopped being a good mother, I never stopped achieving my goals, and I never gave up. It was the moment of realization that all the tears gave me strength, the anxiety gave me courage, and my love for my son and my life never stopped. It was the moment that I realized I thought I had lost my entire life, that I had everything I ever needed cuddled up in my lap and in my heart.

Holly, 26, USA

CHAPTER 17

THE HEALING LOTUS

Here we are at a crossroads. You can continue to look at grief as something that is dark and causes suffering. Something you desire to avoid and run from. Or you can start to see the opportunity to create a lotus from your healing. This means giving yourself the time and space to do the healing work so that you grow from the pain and loss. Grow from the old expectations of how you thought life should go into an openness of how life is. Recognize that positive and negative events will happen to all of us and how we choose to see them is the driver for the type of experience.

When we stay stuck in our own mud, we can't see the roots that are growing. We can't see the bud that is forming. We can't see the color of the petals as they start to release. When we allow that mud to be the catalyst for our growth and approach it with the mindset of "What are you here to teach me?" then we are transformed and can go on the full journey of grief healing. We witness ourselves growing into a beautiful lotus.

Notice though, there is still mud and there is still the need to grow. This means experiencing grief will not feel good. In fact, it's not meant to. In order for it to be a beautiful catalyst for our growth, it needs to be uncomfortable. My best advice is to start getting comfortable with the uncomfortable. Why? Because each time you do so you remind yourself of how strong and capable you are of enduring things that don't feel good.

I want to share with you another analogy that is so powerful to me. Most of us know the life of a caterpillar, especially those who have read *The Very Hungry Caterpillar* by the late Eric Carle. A butterfly lays an egg, the caterpillar later comes out of the egg, eats a ton, builds a cocoon, hangs out in the cocoon while its body transforms into a butterfly, then it pushes its way out and stretches its wings ready to fly. The metaphor of becoming a butterfly is used widely, especially when talking about transforming grief into empowerment. However, we tend to overlook a *big* part of the process. The caterpillar literally turns to mush before becoming the butterfly.

When a caterpillar is ready to transform into a butterfly, it finds a place to hang upside down and does one of two things: either spins a cocoon around itself or molts into a chrysalis. This is where the fun begins. There is a special hormone that isn't released until the caterpillar is safely in a cocoon or chrysalis. If that hormone would be released before this stage, the caterpillar would die. Once this hormone is released, the caterpillar's system basically digests itself.

Another enzyme is released, telling the once caterpillar cells that are now basically mush to create butterfly parts. The magic begins. The butterfly is slowly formed, and when it is done, a new hormone is released, softening the cocoon or chrysalis so the butterfly can push its way out with its legs. When it comes out the wings are wet and need to dry out. Butterflies tend to stay upside down to let this process happen as they open and close their wings. Now it's time to talk about the metaphor of self-transformation from this example.

There is a major event or catalyst that happens, and you instinctively cocoon. You wrap yourself up knowing a change is going to happen. Maybe you only realize this on a subconscious level, but the change will occur whether you like it or not. If you've done past healing work, you know to cocoon or form your chrysalis with healthy support. If you are newer to this work, you may cocoon yourself up with addictive habits or people that don't understand the growth you are about to undertake. The lesson of what actually supports you in your healing is one we all must learn in our healing journey.

As you cocoon, you are transforming grief into empowerment. Your emotions, thoughts, beliefs, opinions, and nature are changing. You are becoming mush, and you cannot rush this. This explains the brain fog we experience in grief as well. We struggle to remember things and think clearly, but it's all normal. It's part of the transformation. We could go further into how we develop into a beautiful butterfly, but my work right now is focused on you in that cocoon. The space where the magic happens. It doesn't feel good at all, but an alchemy is happening. Your pain is being transmuted into power.

What happens though when we try to rush this process, skip a step, or avoid it altogether? Well if we were a caterpillar, we would die. As humans, we get stuck in our grief and we suffer.

We think being in the cocoon of grief causes suffering, but it's actually when we try to control the process that we cause ourselves more problems. Your cocoon is so powerful. It is where the new you is formed. It's not a process to rush or try to skip over important details. You can't fly with only one wing. You can't survive inside the cocoon forever.

When we decondition or re-write the old beliefs that we need instant gratification when something negative happens in order to put a bandage on it we get more comfortable with the uncomfortable. It's ok to have a gummy bear occasionally during a difficult time, but make sure you don't let it turn into a bad habit. How can you be mindful of this? Make time for your grief journey, and when you find yourself coping with things that you have to justify to yourself, that's your warning. The slippery slope of an alcoholic drink to "unwind" or "relax" at the end of the day can then lead to having a drink to feel less of the emotions of grief, to cut the "edge" off the magnitude of what you are feeling. This becomes your gummy bear and hurts your healing process. You begin to equate alcohol, or your chosen escape addiction, with feeling better.

Your personal grief healing process will be unique to you. The catalyst for mine was losing my mom, but the work I needed to do dated back to my childhood and involved a variety of situations. Don't be surprised if you notice you have a lot of past healing work to do too. It's totally normal, and even once you've worked on it, you will probably revisit it again at some point. I like to think of any type of healing work as peeling an onion. Each layer you peel back reveals more and sets you free of the layer before. Oh and you'll shed some tears along the way too!

Now what do you do after learning all this information about grief healing? Well, you get to decide if it's time to turn your past pains and challenges into empowerment and growth. By now you know, this work isn't just about you. It's also to help future generations in your family, neighborhood, community, culture to be more comfortable with grief as well. Do I expect you are going to take up your sword and shield running through the streets yelling, "Grief is real and we all are experiencing it"? No. What I believe will happen is that this book will spark conversations that lead to others being able to better understand their own need for healing. You might give this book as a gift to those in grief who need support or who have been weighed down by the baggage of years of pain and trauma. The lessons in this book will guide you to respond differently in the future to events, which will cause a chain reaction, much like throwing a small rock into a pond. The ripples extend outward, and the impact is far greater than you can see.

YOUR HEALING JOURNEY TOOLS

The first thing I would ask you to do is think about what type of support you need or want when entering your grief journey. Is it seeking support from a counselor, coach, guide, or healer? Is it talking to a close friend or family member and allowing them to check in on you from time to time as you do the work on your own? You get to decide your process and your grief rules. The key is that you know you don't have to do it alone.

Remember the phases of grief are just a guide, not a rule of thumb. They do not go in any particular order and you can experience all of them in a day, in a moment. It is a rollercoaster experience when that occurs, but it happens. You may find new names for the phases so they better fit your experience or even add your own in as well. You create your grief process and with it how you classify things.

There are tools in this book for you to use, but I want to give you a few more. The first one involves time. You will need to set aside time to do this work. I find often people think they need hours; however, it's much like a relationship. You only need about fifteen minutes a day. Completely do-able, right? When we carve out a small amount of time each day, it reminds us that having a relationship with our grief and doing the healing work is completely manageable in everyday life. We can always work on it for longer than fifteen minutes, but I use this daily timeframe to make it more realistic in the beginning.

What should you do in those fifteen minutes? Here's your second tool: close your eyes, take deep breaths, and allow your focus to drop from your thoughts and mind down into your heart. I like to literally imagine warmth or light where my heart is to help my focus go there. Then ask yourself internally or out loud, "Where is my grief today?" Take some time to just feel what comes up, listen to what messages you experience, see what symbols come to mind, and then get to journaling it all out.

The third tool is a journal. Get yourself a journal that brings you a sense of comfort or joy. Carry it around with you because you never know when a layer of the onion wants to show itself. Write in it after you meditate like the example above. Keep a log of memories or dreams that show up that seem important. I was once folding clothes listening to a podcast on entrepreneurship, and a grief memory showed itself in full glory with emotions attached to it and all. I was thrown off by the timing of this memory but realized that when we give our minds permission to start processing the past, older grief memories will pop up at any time. I don't share that to scare you but to emphasize the importance of a journal or notes section of your phone for those moments. A journal is also a great way to track your progress as well.

These three tools will get you started on your grief healing journey and help you navigate the mud of emotions that you may experience. Trust the process. Remember it's like a plant. You water it and keep it by the sun because you know it will eventually grow where you can see it. The funny thing is it's always growing even when you don't see it.

> "There came a time when the risk to remain tight in the bud was more painful than the risk it took to blossom." Anais Nin

I don't know about you, but I have noticed that walking through life feeling like a victim or falling prey to escape addiction doesn't make me feel good about myself or my life. I actually find I make worse decisions when in this mindset. The quote above has been such a powerful one in my life, and one that I have shared with clients over the last thirteen years. For me it means, there is a moment in our lives where keeping our old habits and patterns no longer serves us. It actually makes things more challenging and difficult than if we let go and have faith that it is time for us to grow.

When you reflect on the grief work you will do, remember this quote. Write it in your journal as encouragement that what you are doing is so much better for you than the alternative. Sure it won't feel good, but the growth will be less painful than staying stuck. You are not alone. You are among millions who need to do this work, but you have chosen to take a step forward. You have chosen to see what your personal fires look like to decide if you are ready to walk through them. There are countless people in your life who need you to walk through your fire so you can walk out the other side with buckets of water for them. They need you to be able to sit with and empower them, but first you must face your own experiences. As you finish this book, seriously think about what impact your own healing could have in the lives of others around you. It may be that your own healing leads you to be more patient, less reactive, and more kind to those who don't experience positive treatment in their own homes. Or by walking on your grief journey you know exactly what to do to support someone as they are in the heat of their own grief, when they feel the most alone and ready to make a negative decision about their life. Your impact, your ripple in the water, won't be known until you start taking steps forward.

I'll leave you with one last analogy. In the dark mud, the roots secure themselves. A plant develops growing upward through the murky water. The lotus blossom emerges from the darkness, opens, and displays its petals, beautiful and clean. Each night it retreats again into the cloudy water from where it began. Each day it pushes past the surface of the muddy water to show its beauty to the world. The lotus shows us that darkness and light can coexist in a beautiful way. Grief can feel like the muddy, dark waters the lotus must grow in. It's not that grief is bad, but that it feels heavy, clouded, and lonely. Grief is a tool to help us transform into a beautiful flower that is one with the challenges it has experienced. It's a harmony that is only created when we allow ourselves to heal versus fight or ignore our grief. This is what the new face of grief is all about. This is how you transform your pain into empowerment.

RESOURCES

To support you in your grief healing journey I have put together a toolkit to accompany this book.

Check out katierossler.com/toolkit
to get your free resources, which include:

- ✧ The New Face of Grief Workbook
- ✧ Guided Meditations Library
- ✧ 30 Natural Ways to Support You in Your Grief Guide

ACKNOWLEDGMENTS

To my husband, Max: What a journey we have been on! I can't imagine going on it with anyone else. Thank you for being willing to grow with me and create the life of our dreams. Our daughters are so blessed to have you as their dad. I am grateful for your continued support and love you, my dear.

To my girls: Thank you for letting Mama write. I know you don't fully understand what I am creating yet, but you will one day. This is for your future so you can be free to grow in healthy ways without the boundaries of the "shoulds." I love each of you a million times to the moon and back.

To my family: Y'all have been an amazing support throughout my life. Thank you for being my cheerleaders as I chase my dream. You never have doubted my ability to get where I set my mind to. Thank you for being my roots throughout my life.

To my friends: Ladies, what can I say. You have walked beside me through so much. I always knew you all could make me laugh, sit with me through my darkest moments, and celebrate with me even the smallest wins. Thank you for being my tribe no matter where I am.

To Amie and Jessica: The book publishing process has been such an amazing journey. Thank you for answering my millions of questions and encouraging me all along the way. Your support does not go unnoticed. I couldn't imagine going on this journey the first time with any other rockstars.

To my launch team: Thank you for being by my side to get the word out about *The New Face of Grief.* You all have been so willing to support me and come up with ideas for sharing this important piece of work. Thank you for volunteering your time and energy!

ABOUT THE AUTHOR

Katie Rössler is a licensed professional counselor, transformative grief guide, and speaker from the USA living in Munich, Germany. Her career has taken her on a journey of working in private practice in two countries, residential facilities, homes, and schools, as well as speaking to a variety of corporate and non-profit groups.

After the sudden loss of her mom followed by two miscarriages, she began exploring the world of grief in a new way—as a tool for growth. She discovered methods of transforming pain into empowerment, creating life-changing results.

Katie is a wife, mom of three, and co-founder of Women Entrepreneurs of Munich. She can be found hiking with her family in the mountains and feels at home on her yoga mat.

To work with Katie or have her speak at your next event, go to www.katierossler.com and click on Contact.

Thank you for reading The New Face of Grief!

The best way to help an author is to leave a review on your favorite bookseller site or Goodreads.

Also, I would love to see where in the world you are reading the book, so share a picture of you with the book on your favorite social media platform and tag me in it. You may just get a fun response from me as I love connecting with my community!

www.ingramcontent.com/pod-product-compliance
Ingram Content Group UK Ltd.
Pitfield, Milton Keynes, MK11 3LW, UK
UKHW022003190726
13853UKWH00004B/1697